THE POLITICS
OF PSYCHIATRY
IN REVOLUTIONARY CUBA

CHARLES J. BROWN AND ARMANDO M. LAGO

FREEDOM HOUSE
NEW YORK

OF HUMAN RIGHTS
WASHINGTON

TRANSACTION PUBLISHERS
NEW BRUNSWICK (USA) AND LONDON (UK)

Freedom House
48 E. 21st St.
New York, NY 10010

Of Human Rights
P.O. Box 2160 — Hoya Station
Georgetown University
Washington, DC 20057

Cover design by Emerson, Wajdowicz Studios, Inc., New York.

Library of Congress Cataloging-in-Publication Data

Brown, Charles J.
  The Politics of Psychiatry in Revolutionary Cuba / Charles J.
    Brown and Armando M. Lago
  p. cm.
  Includes bibliographical references and index.
  ISBN 1-56000-020-1 (cloth)
  ISBN 1-56000-585-8 (paper)
  1. Psychiatry — Political aspects — Cuba. 2. Dissenters — Cuba —
  Case studies. 3. Political prisoners — Cuba — Case studies. 4.
  Cuba — Politics and government — Revolution, 1959. I. Lago,
  Armando M. II. Title.
RC449.C9B76   91-7537
                                                        CIP

CONTENTS

PREFACE

ON THE OUTSKIRTS
OF THE EMPIRE

VLADIMIR BUKOVSKY

After reading the documents and testimonies collected in this book, one can feel disgusted and outraged, but not surprised. We have learned long ago that Communist regimes, be they in Vietnam or Cuba, Ethiopia or China, are very much alike: just the sparks, the embers of the huge fire set in the world seventy-four years before. Actually, we would be surprised not to find familiar features in each of them because, to borrow Solzhenitsyn's metaphor, they are like metastases of the same cancer striving to reproduce itself in every part of the globe. Cuba in this regard is unique only by the hasty pace of the disease: it covered in thirty-two years what the Soviet Union achieved in seventy-three. Within a single generation, Cuba advanced from "revolutionary justice" to "socialist legality," from liquidation of "class enemies" to "political re-education" and psychiatric treatment of those "apathetic to socialism."

There are, of course, some differences, too. Strictly speaking, the Cuban regime, where the supreme leader combines in himself Lenin and Stalin, Khrushchev and Brezhnev, does not need to employ psychiatric repression. Invented at the time of "peaceful coexistence," perfected in the era of *detente*, Soviet political psychiatry was intended as a camouflage, allowing the regime to present a more "liberal" image while continuing political repression. In the Cuban context, however, it became just another form of torture. There is no political need for sophisticated diagnostics, no sudden epidemic of "sluggish schizophrenia"[1] among dissidents, no Cuban equivalents of Dr. Lunts and Professor Morozov.[2] Quite a few dissidents were actually diagnosed as sane, or not diagnosed at all, before being sent to the psychiatric gulag and subjected to electric shocks. I imagine even Dr. Lunts would have been outraged seeing such a barbaric application of his elaborate theories.

In short, this is not yet a political abuse of psychiatry as we know it, but rather a bad imitation of it by a not too bright apprentice. One wonders why did the Cuban comrades bother at all to borrow this latest achievement of socialism, if they are not using it properly? Could it be a result of a general Soviet pressure to "liberalize" the Cuban regime and make it more presentable? Or, was it just an instruction from Moscow, routinely dispatched to the outskirts of the empire and wrongly interpreted by a lazy official? Perhaps we will never know.

The fact remains, however, that the first steps toward the political abuse of psychiatry have been made, and further developments are quite likely. Once the political need for a

---

[1] A diagnosis commonly used against Soviet dissidents in order to commit them to mental institutions. The concept of "sluggish" or "creeping" schizophrenia was developed by Professor Andre Snezhnevsky, whose diagnostic framework had a major impact on Soviet psychiatry until his death in 1987. For more on the role of diagnosis in the Cuban model, see pp. 21–22.

[2] Dr. Daniil Lunts and Professor Georgy Morozov are probably the most infamous practicioners of Soviet psychiatric abuse. Lunts systematically perverted his diagnoses of human rights activists and other patients while serving at the notorious Serbsky Institute of Forensic Psychiatry in Moscow. Morozov served as the head of the Serbsky Institute.

more civilized image of the Cuban regime is accepted in Havana, new, better dressed, and cleanly shaven leaders of the Cuban Revolution will appreciate the full potential of the Soviet invention. Then we will hear more and more stories about mental disorders afflicting Cuban society, and it will become much more difficult to cure than now.

Vladimir Bukovsky
Cambridge, England

Vladimir Bukovsky was a leading member of the democratic movement in the Soviet Union during the 1960s and 1970s. He spent twelve years in Soviet prisons, labor camps, and psychiatric hospitals for his work on behalf of human rights, particularly his revelations about the abuse of psychiatry in the Soviet Union. In December 1976, he was released from prison in an exchange for the Chilean Communist leader Luis Corvalán, and expelled to Switzerland. He now resides in Cambridge, England. Mr. Bukovsky is the author of To Build a Castle: My Life as a Dissenter; Letters of a Russian Traveler; *and* The Peace Movement and the Soviet Union. *His most recent work,* USSR: From Utopia to Disaster *was just published in Europe.*

I

OVERVIEW

INTRODUCTION

In 1959, a revolution based on Cuban aspirations for democracy and human rights brought Fidel Castro to power. Within two years of his triumphal entry into Havana, however, Castro had betrayed these principles, imposing a Marxist-Leninist model and initiating the Sovietization of Cuban politics, economics, and society. The constitution, armed forces, media, economy, educational system, labor force, intelligentsia, and every other facet of Cuban society were remodeled to mirror their Soviet counterparts.

Cuban psychiatry did not escape this transformation. Hospitals were nationalized, and psychiatrists became employees of the state. Following their Soviet mentors, Cuban psychiatrists began to function within a strict ideological framework, rejecting Western theories of behavior in favor of those which employ Marxist-Leninist doctrine. And as was the case in the Soviet Union, the Castro regime began to use psychiatry to squelch dissent. Agents of Cuba's State Security apparatus were able to commit anyone in their custody to the forensic ward of a psychiatric institution without consulting a psychiatrist. In other words, State Security began to commit dissidents to mental hospitals for their beliefs.

While Soviet psychiatric abuse has been the focus of world condemnation, its Cuban analog has in large part escaped un-

3

scathed. The Castro regime has mounted an effective public relations campaign, portraying its mental institutions — particularly the Havana Psychiatric Hospital (also known as Mazorra) — as models for other developing nations.[1] In the process, it has attempted to obstruct or hinder efforts by independent experts in the medical, scientific, and human rights communities to investigate conditions in the forensic wards of its hospitals.

For example, the World Psychiatric Association (WPA), which helped lead the fight to expose Soviet psychiatric abuse, has not taken any action against Cuba. According to Fini Schulsinger, the WPA's Secretary-General in 1989, WPA procedural rules "demand that complaints are examined in collaboration with the WPA Member Society in the country in question. As the WPA has no Member Society in Cuba, [it] cannot examine the complaint appropriately."[2] (Cuba's psychiatric association withdrew from the WPA in 1983 in solidarity with the Soviet Union, whose All-Union Society of Psychiatrists and Neuropathologists had withdrawn to avoid expulsion.[3])

Yet the Cuban government has not been able to stem a tide of new allegations of improper psychiatric practices. Fidel Castro's use of the 1980 Mariel boatlift to the United States to deport mental patients resulted in complaints by human rights and psychiatric organizations.[4] International media reports began to appear, including a January 1989 story by Don Schanche of *The Los Angeles Times* on the cases of Jesús Leyva Guerra and José Luis Alvarado Delgado.[5] Of Human Rights, a Georgetown University-based human rights organization, began to compile information on psychiatric abuse in Cuba. Other human rights groups such as Americas Watch and Amnesty International also began to investigate whether the Cuban government was using psychiatry against dissidents.[6] Most importantly, victims of psychiatric abuse began to come forward and speak openly about their experiences.*

This report shows how psychiatry is misused in Cuba for political purposes. It documents twenty-seven cases dating from 1969 to the present.** It includes an overview on the theory and practice of psychiatric abuse, using data from cases to discuss when, where, and how abuse has occurred. Particular attention is paid to conditions within Cuban forensic wards and the misuse of psychotropic drugs and electroconvulsive therapy. Media and human rights organization reports on psychiatric abuse, as well as memoirs by several victims, are included in an Appendix.

The authors are indebted to the hard work of a large number of individuals. Of Human Rights and Freedom House provided financial and administrative support. Richard O'Connell

---

*For the dissidents profiled here, the decision to discuss their experiences was not an easy one. Not unlike victims of sexual assault, victims of psychiatric abuse have suffered a personal humiliation: they fear that public exposure will lead to further ridicule. The tendency in some societies to look down upon or socially ostracize those who seek help for mental illness (much less those who have been confined to a psychiatric hospital) further inhibited some victims. In addition, some investigations were impaired or made impossible because victims were so traumatized that they could not recount their experiences to an interviewer.

**Whenever possible, the authors have verified cases through independent sources. In four cases, however—those of Leandro Hidalgo Pupo, Marcos Miranda Morales, Francisco Tejera Garrido, and Manuel Tejera Garrido—the authors could not determine whether they were confined for their political beliefs or for genuine psychiatric problems. In the case of Emilio Montero Romero, the authors could not corroborate reports of psychiatric abuse through independent accounts. Finally, the case of Samuel Martínez Lara is based in part on his belief that he might have been given psychotropic drugs during an interrogation. However, until the Castro regime allows a thorough and independent investigation into these six cases, the evidence available remains sufficiently compelling to regard these individuals as victims of abuse.

5

provided a small grant that made possible preparation of the original manuscript. Francisco Blanco donated the computer upon which the report was written. Frank Calzon of Freedom House and Christopher Barton, now with the University of Virginia's Center for National Security Law, initiated Of Human Rights' investigation. Frank Calzon in particular has been more than generous with his time; this book could not have been written without his help.

Several individuals helped identify psychiatric abuse cases: Ricardo Bofill of the Cuban Committee for Human Rights; Ramón Cernuda of the Coordinating Committee of Human Rights Organizations in Cuba; Guillermo Estévez of the International Rescue Committee; Mary Jane Camejo at Americas Watch; Rona Weitz of Amnesty International; as well as Roberto Valero, Luis Zúñiga, Andrés Solares, Rafael Saumell, and Julio Vento.

Paul Chodoff, M.D., was kind enough to review the manuscript and make several suggestions. Four other psychiatrists also reviewed the manuscript: Marcelino Feal, M.D., of Miami; Alberto González Acevedo, M.D., of Columbia, South Carolina; Fernando J. Milanés, M.D., of Miami; and Ramona Paneque Abed, M.D., of Miami. Neither they nor anyone mentioned here are in any way responsible for the book or any errors it may contain.

Lourdes Meluza of WLTV-TV, Miami, allowed the use of her news series on psychiatric abuse. Dr. Marcelino Miyares of Times Square Studios provided resources for the transcription and reproduction of the series, enabling its distribution to over one hundred prominent psychiatrists throughout the world. Ken Hughes permitted access to his drawings of the interior of the Havana Psychiatric Hospital originally done for the news series. Alice Conde Martínez, Ricardo Donate, Lilian Sotolongo Dorka, and Richard O'Connell, Jr. helped translate materials. Diego

Roqué, Ricardo Donate, Silvia Zimmerman, Adolfo Rivero, and Oilda del Castillo helped compile casework material. Alicia Roqué, José Alonso, Barbara Futterman, Scott Banville, Eric Singer, Manuel Tellechea, and Vicki Thomas read the manuscript and offered suggestions. Mark Wolkenfeld, Scott Bramson, and Pei Koay helped prepare the manuscript for publication. Ludmilla Thorne, Director of Soviet Studies at Freedom House, reviewed the preface and provided explanatory footnotes where necessary. Christopher Ralph, Sabrina Ousmaal, Richard O'Connell, Jr., Aphrodite Leinas, Jane Shaver, and Andrea Pruitt served as research assistants.

Finally, the authors want to thank those former political prisoners who had the courage to step forward and tell their own stories of psychiatric abuse, as well as the families of those who could not speak for themselves. Their determination to speak out will help bring an end to this ongoing tragedy.

It is both ironic and tragic that at a time when a growing number of Soviet psychiatrists are working from below to eliminate the abuses of Soviet psychiatry and an independent Soviet psychiatric association has been admitted to the World Psychiatric Association, the Castro regime continues to use psychiatric techniques against its opponents. The authors hope that this report will help mobilize international public opinion as well as the world psychiatric and human rights communities in order to pressure the Cuban government to stop this terrible practice.

Notes

1. For an example of how Cuba portrays its psychiatric hospitals, see Patricia Grogg, "Builders of Hope," *Cuba International,* 1/89, pp. 26–29. *Cuba International* is published by the Cuban government for international distribution to the general public. It is similar in design and editorial approach to the Soviet publication, *Soviet Life.* For a report that accepts Havana's portrayal of psychiatry in Cuba, see "Public Health and Psychiatric Care in Cuba: A Personal Report," Dr. Alexander Gralnick's

unpublished memoir of his 1987 visit to Cuba. The Medical Director of High Point Psychiatric Hospital in Port Chester, New York, Gralnick visited two psychiatric units of general hospitals as well as the Havana Psychiatric Hospital. He praised the Cuban authorities and described his tour as "the highlight of my stay in Cuba." However, he openly admits that he did not tour the forensic psychiatry wards (pp. 11–13). It is in these wards that most abuse allegedly occurs.

2. See the 20 February 1989 letter from Fini Schulsinger, M.D., Secretary-General of the World Psychiatric Association, to Eusebio Mujal-Leon, Project Coordinator, Of Human Rights, reprinted in the Appendix on p. 184.

3. For more information on the Soviet withdrawal from the WPA, see the statement by Carl Gershman, United States Representative to the Third Committee, on Items 94 and 97, Human Rights and Scientific and Technological Developments and Torture and Other Cruel, Inhuman or Degrading Treatment or Punishment, United Nations, Press Release USUN 157-(83), 25 November 1983, and "Should the Soviet Psychiatric Association Return to the World Psychiatric Association?" pamphlet (Amsterdam: International Association on the Political Use of Psychiatry, 1989).

4. See "Cuba Dumped Mental Patients on U.S., Psychiatrists Charge," *The Washington Post,* 14 October 1980.

5. Don Schanche, "Cuban Rights Crackdown, Psychiatric Abuses Told," *The Los Angeles Times,* 12 January 1989. The article is reprinted in the Appendix on pp. 123–128.

6. See Amnesty International, *Cuba: Recent Developments Affecting the Situation of Political Prisoners and the Use of the Death Penalty* (New York: Amensty International, 1988), pp. 24–25; Mary Jane Camejo, *Human Rights in Cuba: The Need to Sustain the Pressure* (New York: Americas Watch, 1989), pp. 86–88; and Amnesty International, *Cuba: The Human Rights Situation* (London: Amnesty International, 1990), pp. 22–23. All three are reprinted in the Appendix on pp. 133–135; pp. 130–132, and pp. 181–183 respectively.

A NEW FORM
OF DANGEROUSNESS

In order to understand how psychiatry is used for political purposes in Cuba, it is necessary to review the relationship between psychiatry, political dissidence, and Cuban theories of criminal behavior and deviance.[1] After the 1959 Revolution, Cuban authorities used Marxist-Leninist doctrine to develop a criminal code similar to those found in the Soviet Union and other socialist states. Many crimes were redefined as political acts. The burglary of a neighborhood store, for example, became the theft of state property, "an attack against the right of the workers and families in the neighborhood to acquire consumer goods."[2] Thousands were tried and convicted of "counterrevolutionary" crimes "against the security of the state."[3] According to a 1986 Amnesty International report, sentences "were harsh, often [for] as much as sixty or ninety years. . . . [H]undreds of political prisoners were sentenced to death by Revolutionary Tribunals and executed by firing squads."[4]

In January 1979, the Cuban government adopted a new criminal code, redefining many political acts as common crimes and dividing crime into twelve categories of offenses.* While

---

*The twelve categories are crimes against state security (political crimes); crimes against public order; crimes against the administration of justice; crimes against collective security; crimes against the national and popular economy; crimes against the public trust; crimes against life and physical

9

espionage and "enemy propaganda" continued to be described as "political" acts, "the abuse of religious freedom," "illegal exit from the country," and "illegal meetings" were redefined as common crimes. The Castro regime thus was able to reclassify large numbers of political prisoners as common criminals, reducing dramatically the official number of political prisoners in Cuban jails.[5]**

As was the case in pre-*glasnost* Soviet Union and Communist Eastern Europe, Cuban criminal theory holds that capitalism is the cause of most criminal behavior. In capitalist societies, crime represents collective and/or individual rebellion from the repressive economic policies of the ruling classes; by abolishing private enterprise, socialism abolishes the basis for criminality. In socialist states such as Cuba, crime is an unnatural condition caused by the continued presence of residual capitalism, "the product of negative and non-socialist elements in Marxist societies."[7]

Only by "re-educating" the criminal in the ways of socialism can his or her deviance be ended.[8] The primary purpose of incarceration therefore is not punishment, but re-education:

> the main function of the penitentiary institutions in Cuba is to correct and re-educate the convicts in work habits, the strict observance of law, and respect for social living conventions, to prevent them from perpetrating new crimes.[9]

Re-education should be achieved through "socially useful" work "according to a. . . regime similar to that applicable to all work-

---

well-being; crimes against individual rights; crimes against labor; crimes against the normal development of sexual relations and against the family, children, and adolescents; crimes against honor; and crimes against state property. For more details, see Luis Salas, *Social Control and Deviance in Cuba* (New York: Praeger, 1979), pp. 43-115.

**This was a purely administrative measure; only the *number* of prisoners that Cuba was willing to classify as "political" actually changed.

ers in the country."[10] Once re-educated, the prisoner could become a valuable and productive member of society.

How then does Cuban criminal theory explain *recidivist* behavior, particularly recidivist political behavior? Shouldn't criminals be useful citizens of society once they have been re-educated? Cuban criminology attempts to "explain" such "aberrations" in two ways: first, some criminal behavior is the product of external and internal counterrevolutionary attempts to corrupt Cuban society; second, a small percentage of crimes — particularly those that could be classified as political — are the products of pathological and dysfunctional minds.[11] In other words, those who continue to act in a manner contrary to the will of the regime are either agents of a foreign power or mentally ill.

Such a conceptualization has enabled the Cuban government to redefine some "recidivist" political activity as a form of mental illness. As a result, the State Security apparatus has asserted control over the diagnostic process in political cases. Although forensic wards in Cuban psychiatric hospitals theoretically are under the joint control of State Security agents from the Ministry of Interior and physicians from the Ministry of Public Health, they are in reality little more than part of the punishment apparatus of the secret police. Psychiatry has become a tool of state repression.

This practice did not become institutionalized without some objection from the Cuban psychiatric community. During a 1963 National Conference on Psychiatry at the Havana Psychiatric Hospital (Mazorra), Julio Feijóo, M.D., protested this usurpation of diagnostic procedure:

> Currently, we have two criteria of dangerousness. One. . . defines dangerousness as a morbid presupposition, congenital or acquired by habit, as a result of which. . . the individual has a propensity to commit a crime. . . . But last year. . . a decree was published where the Minister of Interior can de-

11

> clare the dangerousness of a person without [first] obtaining
> medical advice. . . . Thus we find ourselves, at this moment,
> facing two totally different concepts of dangerousness. . . .
> How can it be that in Cuba the rule is, at this moment, that
> decisions of dangerousness can be made on the basis of a
> strictly social investigation without resort to psychological
> evaluations? My question then is: is there a new form of dan-
> gerousness?[12]

Despite the objections of Dr. Feijóo and others, State Security
wrested control of the diagnostic process away from psychiatrists
in those cases involving political dissent. Psychiatrists must cooperate with State Security investigations or face reprisals and arrest.

THE VICTIMS: AN OVERVIEW

The only common denominator among the twenty-seven victims* profiled in this report is that they were confined by the Castro
regime to psychiatric hospitals as a result of their political con-
victions. In fact, it is clear from the evidence that those who practice psychiatric abuse in Cuba have been quite egalitarian in their
approach. Age has not been a factor: José Luis Alvarado Delgado
was sixteen when he was committed, while Eugenio de Sosa Chabau was sixty-one (Table One).[13] Occupation also has had little
to do with confinement, as workers and students have been committed as often as professionals and artists (Table Two). Although
none of the case histories in this report involve women, there have
been allegations of abuse in women's psychiatric wards.**

---

*Four new cases (Rafael Saumell, Oscar Peña, Juan Barzaga, and Luis Al-
berto Pita) came to light as this report went to press. Although brief de-
scriptions of the cases are included, it was not possible to incorporate them
into the overview.

**While the authors did investigate reports of women who allegedly suffered
psychiatric abuse, there was not adequate documentation to include their
cases in this report.

Mental stability also has had little to do with internment: those who are healthy, those with low-grade mental illnesses, and those with illnesses severe enough to require institutionalization all have been among the victims. It is important to emphasize that the issue of psychiatric abuse has little to do with any individual's relative mental health. To quote the late Andrei Sakharov, the critical issue is *"any* use of psychiatry for political or ideological purposes, and not just those cases when mentally healthy individuals are forcibly confined to psychiatric hospitals."[14]

Age Group	Number of Cases
15–20	5
21–25	4
26–30	1
31–35	4
36–40	4
41–45	3
46–50	2
51–65	2

Table One: *Age Distribution (at Internment) of Psychiatric Abuse Cases*

It is possible to divide the twenty-seven cases into four types of abuse:

1. *Dissidents with no prior history of mental illness confined to wards of a psychiatric hospital usually reserved for the criminally insane.* Commitment usually comes as part of the interrogation process and is for the purpose of demoralizing and terrifying the dissident.

2. *Dissidents with no prior history of mental illness given electroconvulsive therapy (ECT), heavy doses of psychotropic drugs, or both as punishment for political behavior.* Such treatment is used to terrorize the dissident into cooperating with his captors; at times it serves to punish the dissident for specific behavior.

3. *Dissidents with low-grade mental illnesses who are subjected to electroconvulsive therapy, heavy doses of psychotropic drugs,*

13

or both as punishment for political behavior. Such treatments are contrary to standard therapeutic procedure or are far above recommended dosage for low-grade mental illness.

4. *Mentally ill individuals whose rights as patients have been abused as a result of their political beliefs.* Some dissidents interned in psychiatric hospitals do have a history of mental illness. Their illnesses

Managerial & Professional	9
Business Executive	1
Physician	2
Engineer	2
Computer Scientist	1
Teacher	3
Artistic and Cultural	**6**
Musician	1
Writer	3
Graphic Designer	1
Filmmaker	1
Skilled & Unskilled Labor	**4**
Seaman	1
Truck Driver	1
Auto Mechanic	1
Farmer *(campesino)*	1
Students	**5**
Unknown	**3**

Table Two: *Occupations (at Internment) of Psychiatric Abuse Victims*

neither explain nor justify the large doses of ECT and psychotropic drugs or the barbaric conditions under which they were administered. It also does not explain or justify cases where genuinely mentally ill individuals were denied treatment as a result of their political beliefs.

EVENTS LEADING TO CONFINEMENT

According to their own testimony as well as that of independent observers, almost every victim profiled in this report was arrested by State Security agents and charged with actions contrary to the interests of the regime (Table Three).[*]

---

[*]The exception is Marcos Miranda Morales, who, although a dissident, was not arrested. He originally was confined to the Enrique Cabrera General Teach-

Most dissidents were taken to State Security headquarters at *Villa Marista** in Havana and subjected to prolonged periods of interrogation. On occasion, interrogators borrowed techniques from the field of psychiatry, including psychotropic drugs and electroshock.

According to Cuban law, those detained by State Security can be referred to psychiatric hospitals for testing in order to determine whether they are fit to stand trial.[15] In September 1988, General Manuel Fernández Crespo, Deputy Minister of the Interior and Chief of the Department of State Security (*Departamento de Seguridad del Estado*), told a delegation from the United Nations Commission on Human Rights that State Security could detain the accused in *Villa Marista* with the full knowledge of his or her relatives for thirty days. If a detainee "showed signs of mental disturbances" he or she "immediately [was] sent to the psychiatric hospital for observation." Psychiatric evaluation could last "for a maximum of thirty days," after which the prisoner would be returned to *Villa Marista*.[16]

These assertions are contrary to the facts. Since the Castro regime suspended the writ of *habeas corpus*, there has been no legal recourse by which the accused or his family can challenge any kind of detention after thirty days.[17] Furthermore, transfer to psychiatric hospitals has occurred even in cases where mental illness is not suspected.[18] State Security agents use the threat of transfer to intimidate the detainee into cooperating.[19] In only a few of the cases included in this report did confinement occur after trial and sentencing.[20] In most cases, a State Security agent — *not* a qualified psychiatrist — ordered the commitment.

---

ing Hospital for symptoms of stress. He was subjected to abuse after a psychiatrist accused him of faking his symptoms. For the details of his case, see pp 112–113.

Villa Marista, also known as the Center for State Security Investigations, is a former Marist Brothers high school nationalized by the Castro regime and converted into the Havana headquarters and interrogation center of State Security.

Counterrevolutionary propaganda	6
Trying to leave country illegally	7
Anti-regime activity	10
Contempt for the regime	2
Refusal to serve in armed forces	3
Illegal currency exchange	1
Actions against chief of diplomatic representation	1
Alleged plots to murder Castro	5
Clandestine printing	2
Espionage	1
Hijacking	1
Taking photos without a license	1
Illegal association	1

Table Three: *Charges brought against dissidents after arrest(s)*

LENGTH OF CONFINEMENT

Dissidents have been held in psychiatric hospitals for as long as five years and for as briefly as one day (Table Four). There appears to be a link between the length of and the reasons for confinement: in cases where the dissident was interned for less than three months, confinement almost always was part of the interrogation process. In other words, most dissidents were confined for short periods of time in order to terrify them into cooperating with their interrogators, and not in order to determine their relative mental health.

LOCATION AND CONDITIONS OF CONFINEMENT

In almost every case, dissidents were confined to wards for the criminally insane. Eduardo Bernabé Ordaz Ducungé,

M.D., the director of the Havana Psychiatric Hospital, has noted that this is standard practice:

> We do not have political prisoners and common prisoners [in wards for the criminally insane]: all are inmates, interned

Name	Total Stay	Times Held
Samuel Martínez Lara	1 day	1
Juan Manuel García Cao	2 days	1
Andrés Solares Teseiro	3 days	1
Emilio Montero Romero	7 days	1
Manuel Tejera Garrido	7 days	1
Silvio Aguila Yanes	7 days	1
Ariel Hidalgo Guillén	10 days	1
Orlando Polo González	12 days	1
Amaro Gómez Boix	14 days	1
F. Mario Zaldívar Batista	15 days	1
José Morales Rodríguez	18 days	1
Esteban Cárdenas Junquera	24 days	1
José Luis Alvarado Delgado	1 month	2
Eduardo Yanes Santana	1 month	2
J. Roberto Bahamonde Masot	40 days	3
Julio Soto Angurel	6 weeks	1
Juan Peñate Fernández	48 days	1
Marcos Miranda Morales	2 months	1
Gualdo Hidalgo Portilla	69 days	1
Orestes Martínez Haydar	4 months	1
Angel Quiñones González	12 months	1
Jesús Leyva Guerra	39 months	7
Nicolás Guillén Landrián	5 years	4
Julio Vento Roberes	5 years	1
Leandro Hidalgo Pupo	still confined	1
Francisco Tejera Garrido	unknown	1

Table Four: *Length of Confinement in Psychiatric Wards and Number of Times Confined*

through a judicial process, some under common penal processes, others for political crimes.[21]

Data from Cuban psychiatric journals have confirmed that political dissidents are confined in Cuban psychiatric hospitals. Using data from a 1984 study of disciplinary infractions at the Córdova forensic ward for women at the Havana Psychiatric Hospital (Mazorra), it is possible to determine that one percent of all women interned in the ward had been convicted of crimes against state security and

Name	ECT	Drugs	None	Unknown
Silvio Aguila Yanes	4	x		
José Luis Alvarado	3	x		
Roberto Bahamonde Masot	8	x		
Esteban Cárdenas Junquera		x		
Eugenio de Sosa Chabau	14	x		
Juan Manuel García Cao		x		
Amaro Gómez Boix		x		
Nicolás Guillén Landrián	20	x		
Ariel Hidalgo Guillén			x	
Gualdo Hidalgo Portilla	8–12	x		
Leandro Hidalgo Pupo				x
Jesús Leyva Guerra	24	x		
Orestes Martínez Haydar	16	x		
Samuel Martínez Lara				x
Marcos Miranda Morales	7			
Emilio Montero Romero				x
José Morales Rodríguez	14	x		
Juan Peñate Fernández			x	
Orlando Polo González			x	
Angel Quiñones González				x
Andrés Solares Teseiro			x	
Julio Soto Angurel				x
Manuel Tejera Garrido				x
Francisco Tejera Garrido				x
Julio Vento Roberes	16	x		
Eduardo Yanes Santana		x		
F. Mario Zaldívar Batista		x		

Table Five: *Use of ECT and Psychotropic Drugs*

18

an additional 3.6 percent had been found guilty of crimes against the public order.[22] The same study also noted that the Department of State Security was among the organizations that remit internees to psychiatric hospitals.[23] Data from a 1980 study of patients experiencing depression who were interned at the Havana Psychiatric Hospital can be used to estimate that 6.3 percent of patients questioned had encountered problems with authorities as a result of their political beliefs.[24]

Most dissidents were committed to the Carbó-Serviá and Castellanos wards of the Havana Psychiatric Hospital (Mazorra).[*] There are reports of abuse at other hospitals, however, including the Gustavo Machín Psychiatric Hospital (Jagua) in Santiago de Cuba, the Enrique Cabrera General Teaching Hospital in Havana, the Combinado del Este Prison Hospital in Havana and the Habana del Este Naval Hospital in Santa María del Mar, Havana province.

In March 1988, a delegation from Amnesty International was able to gain access to the Carbó-Serviá ward of the Havana Psychiatric Hospital (Mazorra). They noted that the ward

> consisted of a poorly-lit main room with several rows of about 90 closely-packed beds, a dining room with cement tables and benches, a sick bay, and several individual interviewing cubicles. The director of the unit explained that if an inmate showed signs of agitation, they [sic] would be taken to the sick bay, strapped to a bed and sedated.[25]

Amnesty complained that "people not suffering from any psychological disorder are held together with violent psychopaths and seriously disturbed people, making their stay there a very traumatic experience and leaving the practice open to abuse." Amnesty described Carbó-Serviá as "an old, dark building, contrast[ing] sharply with the rest of the hospital premises, which

---

[*] Havana Psychiatric Hospital also is known as the National Psychiatric Hospital. Mazorra was its pre-revolutionary name.

are bright and modern." The delegation was told that "a brand new forensic psychiatry unit is being built where conditions and facilities would be considerably improved."[26]

In September 1988, a delegation from the United Nations Commission on Human Rights was allowed to visit Carbó-Serviá. The delegation's report states that "the Director [of the Havana Psychiatric Hospital] recognized the need for more mod-

Patient	Diagnosis
Silvio Aguila Yanes	Unknown
José Luis Alvarado Delgado	Sane
Roberto Bahamonde Masot	Paranoia
Esteban Cárdenas Junquera	Psychotic
Eugenio de Sosa Chabau	None
Juan Manuel García Cao	Sane
Amaro Gómez Boix	Sane
Nicolás Guillén Landrián	Unknown
Ariel Hidalgo Guillén	Sane
Gualdo Hidalgo Portilla	Paranoid schizophrenia
Leandro Hidalgo Pupo	Paranoid schizophrenia
Jesús Leyva Guerra	Paranoid schizophrenia
Orestes Martínez Haydar	Paranoid schizophrenia
Samuel Martínez Lara	Psychopathy
Marcos Miranda Morales	Stress
Emilio Montero Romero	None
José Morales Rodríguez	Unknown
Juan Peñate Fernández	None
Orlando Polo González	Chronic paranoia
Angel Quiñones González	Unknown
Andrés Solares Teseiro	None
Julio Soto Angurel	Unknown
Manuel Tejera Garrido	Apathetic to socialism
Francisco Tejera Garrido	Unknown
Julio Vento Roberes	Acute paranoia
Eduardo Yanes Santana	Unknown
F. Mario Zaldívar Batista	Anxiety

Table Six: *Diagnoses of Victims of Psychiatric Abuse*

ern premises for this unit and expressed hope that work on their construction would begin shortly."[27]

However, dissidents confined to the forensic wards paint a much grimmer picture: forced confinement during the day to an outdoor area more like a cage than a courtyard;[28] dangerously unsanitary conditions;[29] beatings and rapes at the hands of guards, officers, or criminally insane inmates;[30] excessive doses of psychotropic drugs, sometimes administered in pill form,[31] sometimes mixed in with the food;[32] the use of criminally insane inmates as orderlies;[33] and torture in the form of unnecessary electroconvulsive therapy (ECT).[34] Most of the dissidents interviewed said that they feared for their personal safety. Several witnessed the death of fellow inmates.[35] At least one dissident was murdered.[36]

DIAGNOSIS

Earlier studies of psychiatric abuse in the Soviet Union have emphasized a diagnosis of "sluggish schizophrenia" in cases involving dissidents.[37] The sluggish schizophrenic, usually middle-aged and male, is able to function in a social setting. Symptoms common to other forms of schizophrenia, such as withdrawal, bizarre behavior, or a poor perception of reality, are not exhibited. The patient appears sane. His illness manifests itself only through such "aberrant" behavior as "overvalu[ing] his own importance" and "exhibit[ing] grandiose ideas of reforming the world."[38] Since sluggish schizophrenia develops slowly, only a psychiatrist can recognize and diagnose its presence. Not recognized as a legitimate diagnosis in the West, sluggish schizophrenia was used by Soviet psychiatrists to justify the confinement of sane dissidents to psychiatric hospitals.

Although there are no reports of Cuban psychiatrists using a diagnosis of sluggish schizophrenia to justify the confinement of dissidents to psychiatric hospitals, Julio Vento Roberes was diagnosed as suffering from "delusions that he was a defender

21

of human rights."[39] Four other dissidents were diagnosed as suffering from paranoid schizophrenia.[40]

In only twelve of twenty-seven cases were dissidents diagnosed as mentally ill (Table Six). One of these was diagnosed as "apathetic to socialism."[41] Four were not diagnosed.[42] Four others were told by a psychiatrist that they were sane, *and then returned to the psychiatric hospital.*[43] In seven cases, there was not enough evidence to determine whether a diagnosis was made.[44]

Although the reasons for this lack of uniformity in diagnosis are unclear, some educated guesses are possible. First, the small number of cases makes it impossible to derive firm conclusions supported by statistical inference methods; as more cases are documented, a more consistent pattern may develop. Second, unlike the Soviets, Cuban authorities may be uninterested in using specific psychiatric terminology to justify confinement. Third, State Security confines dissidents to mental institutions in order to terrorize them, not to cure them. Diagnosis therefore may be superfluous.

THE ABUSE OF ELECTROCONVULSIVE THERAPY (ECT)

Many psychiatrists recognize electroconvulsive therapy, also known as electroshock therapy or ECT, as appropriate treatment for some mental illnesses.[45] ECT usually is administered in a hospital setting to a patient under anesthesia who has been given muscle relaxants to reduce the risk of injury.[46] The standard treatment involves six to nine sessions, administered three times a week.[47] In some cases, short-term memory loss is a potential but reversible side effect.[48]

Dictatorships throughout the world have adapted these techniques to torture opponents. Cuba is no exception. Cuban authorities have used electroshock in the forensic wards of psychiatric hospitals to punish past actions and control current behavior. Eleven of the twenty-seven victims of psychiatric abuse profiled in this report were forced to undergo electroconvulsive therapy (Table Five).[49] Another three were forced to watch while electroshocks were administered to fellow inmates.[50] ECT was dispensed liberally, almost always without the presence of a physician.[51] It is likely that in some cases, patients were given ECT while under the influence of psychotropic drugs.[52] Dissidents have been forced to undergo as few as three and as many as twenty-four sessions of ECT. Neither length of stay nor diagnosis played a role in determining whether ECT was administered.[53] Neither the patient nor his family were notified of the reasons for the use of ECT, nor were they given the opportunity to refuse the procedure. There were not any follow-up evaluations in order to determine whether ECT accomplished the desired therapeutic effect.[54]

According to the testimony of those who were given ECT, the victim usually is strapped to or held down on a damp floor,[55] which at times is covered with the vomit, urine, and excrement of earlier victims.[56] He then is doused with cold water in order to improve conductivity.[57] Contrary to standard procedure, he is given neither anesthesia nor muscle relaxants.[58] Sometimes the rubber bit designed to prevent him from biting or swallowing his tongue is forgotten.[59] Electrodes are attached to his head,[60] his body,[61] and sometimes his testicles.[62] Before the session begins, other inmates are brought into the room and are forced to watch.[63] Electroshocks are applied until the victim goes into convulsions and becomes unconscious.[64] Several dissidents have reported that they suffered short-term memory loss as a result of these sessions.[65]

INDISCRIMINATE ABUSE OF PSYCHOTROPIC DRUGS

Psychotropic drugs, also known as anti-psychotics or neuroleptics, have become the treatment of choice in modern psychiatry for certain mental illnesses, including schizophrenia.[66] In most cases, anti-psychotics act on the schizophrenic's central nervous system to reduce anxiety and excitement. Long-term use usually helps control and eventually eliminate hallucinations in most patients.[67]

Phenothiazines are among the most commonly used antipsychotics.[68] Since they almost exclusively are the drugs used against dissidents in Cuba, this report limits its discussion to this class of drugs. In the West, dosage and administration of phenothiazines vary from patient to patient, depending on the severity of the illness and the potential for side effects.[69] They usually are administered orally. Once the patient's symptoms are brought under control, dosage is reduced gradually until a minimum maintenance level is determined.[70]

Use of phenothiazines can cause a variety of side effects, including seizures, high or low blood pressure, exhaustion, blurred vision, fainting, loss of balance, stiffness, weakness in the arms or legs, weight gain, allergic skin reactions, constipation, difficult urination, and nasal congestion.[71] Those who are mentally healthy are more likely to develop side effects at lower dosages than those who are not. In addition, phenothiazines often produce in their users what are known as extrapyramidal effects — interference with the part of the brain responsible for normal movement and coordination. Extrapyramidal effects can include slowness, rigidity, paucity of body movement, tremors, involuntary restlessness, and a condition known as tardive dyskinesia, the involuntary, purposeless movement of certain muscle groups such as the lips, tongue and face.[72] Since chronic use can make this condition irreversible, psychiatrists often try to substitute less harmful treatments.[73]

Since there are risks involved in the use of these drugs, most psychiatrists set dosage carefully, monitor regularly for potential side effects, and prescribe anti-Parkinsonian drugs when appropriate.[74] Most doctors inform prospective users, their families, or both, of the drug's side effects, and often will offer the option of refusing its use.[75]

In Cuba, phenothiazines — particularly chlorpromazine (also known by the brand name thorazine[76]) — have been used extensively on dissidents in psychiatric hospitals. At least fifteen of the twenty-seven individuals profiled in this report were forced to ingest large doses of psychotropic drugs (Table Five).[77] Drugs usually were administered orally in tablet form; those who refused the drug were beaten until they changed their minds.[78] At times, drugs were mixed with food so that dissidents would be unaware that they had ingested a drug until it attacked their central nervous systems. Dissidents then had to choose between eating and being drug-free.[79] Dosage varied, but at least two individuals were forced to ingest five hundred milligrams of chlorpromazine on a regular basis.[80]

Cuban authorities apparently were not concerned that some dissidents developed adverse side effects as a result of the indiscriminate use of phenothiazines. Several dissidents lost control over simple motor functions; several others endured memory losses so severe that they were unable to remember their own name.[81]

In light of their indiscriminate use of medication, their lack of concern over dosage, and their failure to monitor users for adverse side effects, it is clear that Cuban authorities use psychotropic drugs to punish, intimidate and demoralize dissidents rather than to cure them. The Cuban government apparently hopes to coerce dissidents into cooperating with the regime and discontinuing their activities. In addition, Cuban authorities on occasion have allowed members of a dissident's family to see the victim in such a state, hoping they will pressure the dissident to discontinue his activities.

PATIENT RIGHTS[82]

Over the past two decades, much of the world psychiatric community has come to accept the idea that patients in psychiatric hospitals have certain rights, including the right to individualized treatment;[83] the right to a reasonable opportunity to be cured within a reasonable period of time;[84] the right to a humane physical and psychological environment with acceptable standards of hygiene;[85] the right to refuse treatment;[86] the right not to be subjected to experimental treatment without consent;[87] the right to be treated and cared for by an adequately trained staff;[88] and the right to be confined in a manner that guarantees the safety of both the patient and those around him.[89]

None of these rights is respected in the forensic wards of Cuban psychiatric hospitals. Dissident accounts portray conditions incompatible with what is considered appropriate treatment of the mentally ill. Wards such as Carbó-Serviá and Castellanos in the Havana Psychiatric Hospital (Mazorra) are in reality no more than prisons for the criminally insane. They function not to cure inmates, but to confine mentally ill persons found guilty of violent crimes.

From the testimony of the dissidents interviewed for this report, it is clear that staffing of such institutions is haphazard at best. Little or no effort is made to provide adequate daily treatment; inmates are for the most part left to their own devices. Several dissidents have reported that criminally insane inmates serve as orderlies. Others have stated that members of the staff beat and rape inmates, threatening them with electroconvulsive therapy and psychotropic drugs if they do not cooperate.

Inmates in Cuba's wards for the criminally insane do not play a role in their own therapy. Cuban authorities make no effort to individualize treatment to the specific needs of the patient. Dissidents are not allowed to refuse treatment, even when it involves such potentially dangerous procedures as electroconvulsive therapy and the administration of large doses of psychotropic drugs. Those who attempt to refuse treatment are punished.[90] Families also are excluded from therapy, with visits often restricted or even disallowed. In at least two cases, families were not told that the dissident had been confined to the psychiatric hospital.[91]

IS THE ABUSE OF PSYCHIATRY A FORM OF TORTURE?

According to the International Convention against Torture and Other Cruel, Inhuman or Degrading Treatment or Punishment,[92] which was signed by Cuba on 27 January 1986,[93] "torture" can be defined as

> any act by which severe pain or suffering, whether physical or mental, is intentionally inflicted on a person for such purposes as obtaining from him or a third person information or a confession, punishing him for an act he or a third person has committed or is suspected of having committed, or intimidating or coercing him or a third person for any reason based on discrimination of any kind, when such pain or suffering is inflicted by or at the instigation of or with the consent or acquiescence of a public official or other person acting in an official capacity.[94]

For an act to be torture, the state must play a leading role in tolerating and encouraging its practice. As Amnesty International has noted, torture "does not occur simply because individual torturers are sadistic. . . [but because it] is usually part of the state controlled machinery to suppress dissent. Concentrated in the torturer's electrode or syringe is the power and responsibility of the state."[95]

There are several sets of criteria which have been developed to determine whether a given act can be defined as torture. Amnesty International cites four determinants: "the severity of physical or mental pain or suffering caused to the victim, the deliberateness of the act, the fact that the act has a purpose,

27

and the direct or indirect involvement of state officials in the act."[96] Elena O. Nightingale, M.D., Ph.D., the Chair of the American Association for the Advancement of Science (AAAS) Committee on Scientific Freedom and Responsibility, has suggested a more detailed model:

> First, at least two persons are involved — a perpetrator and a victim, and often, though not always, they are face-to-face. Second, the torturer has complete physical control over the victim. This is important because the helplessness of the victim remains with him long after the torture episode is over. Third, pain and suffering are an integral part of torture, but the main purpose is not really pain and suffering, but rather humiliation and breaking of the will. . . . Finally, torture is a purposeful, systematic activity. In addition to breaking the will of the victim. . . . the purpose is not only to destroy the person who is being tortured, but to have that person be a lesson to others so they will not do whatever the government that sanctions torture feels is not in its interests.[97]

Using a synthesis of Amnesty's and Nightingale's criteria, it is possible to determine that psychiatry as practiced against dissidents in Cuba can be defined as torture:

1. At least two persons are involved — a perpetrator and a victim. Often, the victim suffers at the hands of more than one perpetrator: the State Security officer who decides to commit the dissident to the psychiatric institution; the doctor who tells him he is sane but returns him to the ward; the orderly who administers electric shocks or force feeds him psychotropic drugs; the inmates who beat or rape him with the complicity of the hospital staff.

2. The perpetrator has complete physical control over the victim. The victim is confined to a ward for the criminally insane and cannot leave its premises. Psychotropic drugs, electroconvulsive therapy, beatings, and other forms of intimidation are administered without his consent.

3. Severe physical and mental pain and suffering are an integral part of the process. Victims often are beaten or raped. They are forced to ingest psychotropic drugs, which lead to the loss of control of certain muscle functions or of memory, as well as a number of other side effects. They are forced to undergo electroconvulsive therapy without anesthesia or muscle relaxants.

4. The process is deliberate, purposeful, and systematic. Confinement to a psychiatric hospital is one of many techniques used by Cuban State Security agents to assure a successful interrogation. Once confined, techniques vary from case to case. All, however, involve a systematic challenge to the dissident's self-image as sane and whole.

5. The main purpose of the procedure is not inflicting pain and suffering but rather obtaining information or a confession, in the process humiliating the victim and destroying his or her will to resist. Dissidents were threatened with the stigma of being labeled mentally ill if they did not cooperate. Several were warned repeatedly (before being sent to the psychiatric hospital, during their stay, and upon leaving) that they would be confined to the forensic ward until they began to cooperate by confessing to crimes they did not commit. Several were transferred out of the hospital after signing confessions.

6. The process is designed not only to punish the victim but to convince others to reconsider their own dissidence. Dissidents are confined to psychiatric institutions not only to punish them for their own behavior, but also to discourage others. In several cases, Cuban authorities allowed family and friends to see dissidents under the influence of psychotropic drugs or after

29

electroconvulsive therapy so that they would be persuaded to avoid the same "mistakes."

7. *A government or governmental body sanctions the activity; state officials directly or indirectly participate in the procedure.* Hospitals are controlled by the state. The psychiatrists, orderlies, and guards responsible for the administration of unnecessary electroconvulsive therapy, excessive doses of psychotropic drugs, and beatings, are employees of the state. Forensic wards are under the control of the State Security apparatus. The decision to confine a dissident to a forensic ward is made by the State Security apparatus.

What Can Be Done?

From the evidence gathered for this report, it is clear that the Cuban government misuses psychiatry for political purposes. The Cuban government has confined political prisoners to psychiatric hospitals in order to obtain confessions for alleged crimes. The practice continues today: the experiences of Orlando Polo González, Julio Soto Angurel, Jesús Leyva Guerra, Francisco Tejera Garrido, Samuel Martínez Lara, Manuel Tejera Garrido, Angel Tomás Quiñones González, and Leandro Hidalgo Pupo, as well as the new cases made public in December 1990 by Amnesty International, all provide evidence of recent abuse.

Human rights organizations, psychiatric associations, and civic leaders the world over must act to help bring an end to this practice. The World Psychiatric Association should begin an investigation of psychiatric practices in Cuba. If its procedural rules prohibit an investigation, then it should encourage those member organizations with relations with the Cuban psychiatric community to conduct bilateral investigations on their own.

The United Nations Commission on Human Rights, the United Nations Committee on Torture, the Organization of

American States' Interamerican Commission on Human Rights, and the American Psychiatric Association should investigate these allegations. International human rights organizations such as Americas Watch and Amnesty International should open new investigations of Cuban psychiatric practices. Political, intellectual, and religious leaders with access to the Cuban leadership should bring the matter to the attention of Fidel Castro. Only the vocal, outraged expression of international public opinion will force the government of Cuba to bring to an end this barbaric practice.

NOTES

1. The following discussion is based primarily on Luis Salas, *Social Control and Deviance in Cuba* (New York: Praeger, 1979), particularly pp. 127–133 [hereafter cited as Salas].

2. Taken from a 7 January 1976 article in *Granma* (the official newspaper of the Communist Party of Cuba), quoted in Salas, p. 8.

3. Salas, pp. 44–45.

4. Amnesty International, *Political Imprisonment in Cuba* (London: Amnesty International, 1986), p. 1.

5. Salas, pp. 46; p. 62.

6. Salas, pp. 127–8.

7. Salas, p. 130.

8. Salas, p. 129. This theory helps explain the presence of large scale re-education programs in the Cuban penal system as well as the use of negative incentives to persuade political prisoners to submit to re-education.

9. From a Ministry of Justice publication entitled *El Sistema Jurídico Penal en Cuba (The Penal Legal System in Cuba)*, quoted in *Political Imprisonment in Cuba*, p. 3.

31

10. Quoted in *Political Imprisonment in Cuba,* p. 3.

11. A good example of this belief in the connection between criminal behavior and mental illness is a 1959 statement by Nikita Khrushchev: "A crime is a deviation from the generally recognized standards of behaviour, frequently caused by mental disorder. Can there be diseases, nervous disorders among certain people in the Communist society [of the future]? Evidently there can be. If that is so, then there also will be offences which are characteristic of people with abnormal minds. . . . To those who might start calling for opposition to Communism on this 'basis', we say that now, too, there are people who fight against Communism. . . but clearly the mental state of such people is not normal." Taken from a 24 May 1959 article in *Pravda,* quoted in Sidney Bloch and Peter Reddaway, *Russia's Political Hospitals: The Abuse of Psychiatry in the Soviet Union* (London: Victor Gollancz, Ltd., 1977), p. 62. See also Salas, pp. 131–133.

12. "Conferencia Nacional de Instituciones Psiquiátricas," *Revista del Hospital Psiquiátrico de la Habana* IV (April–June 1963): 225–226.

13. See the cases of José Luis Alvarado Delgado and Eugenio de Sosa Chabau.

14. Emphasis from the original. Andrei Sakharov, *Memoirs* (New York: Alfred A. Knopf, 1990), p. 330.

15. Amnesty International, *Cuba: The Human Rights Situation* (London: Amnesty International, December 1990), p. 22.

16. United Nations, Economic and Social Council, Commission on Human Rights, *Consideration of the Report of the Mission which Took Place in Cuba in Accordance with the Commission Decision 1988/106,* Forty-fifth session, Item 11, E/CN.4/1989/46, 21 February 1989, p. 26.

17. A number of sources question the assertion of Cuban authorities that an accused can be held for no more than thirty days. See, for example, United States, Department of State, Bureau of Human Rights and Humanitarian Affairs, *Human Rights in Castro's Cuba* (Washington: Department of State, 20 May 1986), p. 21; and Amnesty International, *Report 1983* (London: Amnesty International, 1983), p. 129.

18. On 6 August 1989, the human rights activists Elizardo Sánchez Santa Cruz and Hubert Jeréz Mariño were arrested. On 24 October, they were transferred from the Combinado del Este prison to the Havana Psychiatric Hospital (Mazorra). On 26 October, they were returned to Combinado del Este. Since little is known of their internment in Mazorra, their cases have not been included in this report. For more on their cases, see Americas Watch, *Cuba: Jailing the Human Rights Movement* (New York: Americas Watch, March 1990), pp. 3–6, and Julia Preston, "Castro's Clamping Down Again," *The Washington Post,* 22 October 1989. For allegations that Cuba has adopted as standard practice the short term confinement of dissidents in psychiatric hospitals, see *Human Rights in Castro's Cuba,* pp. 20–21; and Raymond D. Gastil, editor, *Freedom in the World 1982: Political Rights and Civil Liberties* (New York: Freedom House, 1982), p. 283.

19. In two cases, however, dissidents were sent to a psychiatric hospital to punish them for behavior while in detention. Eduardo Yanes Santana was transferred from a Military Units to Aid Production (UMAP) labor camp to Camagüey Psychiatric Hospital for defying UMAP authority. When Eugenio de Sosa Chabau struck the State Security agent interrogating him, he was beaten and transferred to the Havana Psychiatric Hospital (Mazorra).

20. See, for example, the case of Julio Vento Roberes, who was confined to the Havana Psychiatric Hospital (Mazorra) after being sentenced to five years in prison for enemy propaganda. Vento served his entire sentence in the Carbó-Serviá wing of the Hospital.

21. Comments of Eduardo Bernabé Ordaz Ducungé, M.D., on an article by Arnaldo Torriente Gutiérrez, M.D., "Trabajo Clínico de Observación de Procesados [Clinical Work and Observation of Judicially Processed Patients]," *Revista del Hospital Psiquiátrico de la Habana* V (July–August 1964): 469.

22. Derived from data in Migdalia Soyu, Jorge L. Perera Horta, and Alexis Alonso Rodríguez, "Violaciones Disciplinarias de los Pacientes en el Servicio Psiquiátra Forense [Disciplinary Infractions by Forensic Psychiatric Service Patients]," *Revista del Hospital Psiquiátrico de la Habana* XXV (October–December 1984): 512.

23. Soyu, et. al., p. 513.

24. Derived from data in Ramón C. de las Pozas, Norma Merino, and Luis Calzadilla, "Consideraciones para una Historia Natural de los Cuadros Depresivos [Considerations on a Natural History of Depressive Disorders]," *Revista del Hospital Psiquiátrico de la Habana*, XXI (January–March 1980): 52.

25. Amnesty International, *Cuba: Recent Developments Affecting the Situation of Political Prisoners and the Use of the Death Penalty* (New York: Amnesty International, September 1988), p. 24 [hereafter cited as AI/September 1988].

26. All quotes from AI/September 1988, p. 25. In December 1990, Rona Weitz, Deputy Director of Amnesty International's Washington Office, stated that there was no evidence that a new forensic facility had been built. Amnesty International's December 1990 report confirms that Carbó-Serviá continues to be in use. See Amnesty International, *Cuba: The Human Rights Situation* (London: Amnesty International, December 1990), pp. 22–23, which is reprinted in the Appendix on pp. 181–183.

27. *Consideration of the Report of the Mission which Took Place in Cuba in Accordance with the Commission Decision 1988/106*, pp. 47–48.

28. See, for example, the cases of Ariel Hidalgo Guillén and Amaro Gómez Boix.

29. See, for example, the cases of Javier Roberto Bahamonde Masot; Esteban Cárdenas Junquera; Eugenio de Sosa Chabau; Juan Manuel García Cao; and Ariel Hidalgo Guillén.

30. Dissidents who witnessed beatings or were beaten include Javier Roberto Bahamonde Masot; Esteban Cárdenas Junquera; Eugenio de Sosa Chabau; Juan Manuel García Cao; Ariel Hidalgo Guillén; Orestes Martínez Haydar; Juan Peñate Fernández; Angel Tomás Quiñones González; and Andrés José Solares Teseiro. Dissidents who have alleged that rapes of other inmates occurred include Eugenio de Sosa Chabau; Juan Manuel García Cao; Amaro Gómez Boix; and Ariel Hidalgo Guillén.

31. Dissidents who received psychotropic drugs in pill form include Esteban Cárdenas Junquera; Amaro Gómez Boix; and Jesús Leyva Guerra.

32. Dissidents who received drugs mixed in with their food include José Luis Alvarado Delgado; Eugenio de Sosa Chabau; Juan Manuel García Cao; Eduardo Yanes San-tana; and Orestes Martínez Haydar.

33. Dissidents who witnessed the use of inmates as orderlies or aides include Esteban Cárdenas Junquera; Eugenio de Sosa Chabau; Ariel Hidalgo Guillén; Gualdo Hidalgo Portilla; Orestes Martínez Haydar; Emilio Montero Romero; Eduardo Yanes Santana; and F. Mario Zaldívar Batista.

34. Dissidents who received electroshocks include José Luis Alvarado Delgado (3 sessions of ECT); Javier Roberto Bahamonde Masot (8); Eugenio de Sosa Chabau (14); Nicolás Guillén Landrian (20); Jesús Leyva Guerra (24); Orestes Martínez Haydar (16); Marcos Miranda Morales (7); José Morales Rodríguez (14); Silvio Aguila Yanes (4); Gualdo Hidalgo Portilla (between 8 and 12); and Julio Vento Roberes (16).

35. See, for example, the case of Eugenio de Sosa Chabau, who has stated that during his stay in the Carbó-Serviá wing of the Havana Psychiatric Hospital (Mazorra), five inmates died.

36. In March 1990, the dissident Angel Tomás Quiñones González was murdered in the Carbó-Serviá ward of the Havana Psychiatric Hospital (Mazorra). He had been lynched, his body doused with gasoline and set on fire. Quiñones' mother has accused Cuban authorities of complicity as a result of the unlikely presence of gasoline in a ward for the criminally insane. At the time this book went to press, the Cuban government had not yet responded to these charges.

37. The following discussion of sluggish schizophrenia is derived from Bloch and Reddaway, *Russia's Political Hospitals,* pp. 243–255.

38. *Russia's Political Hospitals,* p. 247. At times such diagnoses have bordered on the absurd. When Soviet biologist and human rights activist Zhores Medvedev was diagnosed as schizophrenic, his interest in the disparate fields of biology and political science was cited as evidence of his "split personality." See Zhores Medvedev and Roy Medvedev, *A Question of Madness: Repression by Psychiatry in the Soviet Union* (New York: Random House, 1971), pp. 45–46. See also Andrei Sakharov, *Memoirs,* p. 310.

39. See the case of Julio Vento Roberes.

40. See the cases of Leandro Hidalgo Pupo, Jesús Leyva Guerra, Gualdo Hidalgo Portilla, and Orestes Martínez Haydar.

41. See the case of Manuel Tejera Garrido.

42. See the cases of Eugenio de Sosa Chabau, Emilio Montero Romero, Juan Peñate Fernández, and Andrés José Solares Teseiro.

43. See the cases of José Luis Alvarado Delgado; Juan Manuel García Cao; Amaro Gómez Boix; and Ariel Hidalgo Guillén.

44. See the cases of Silvio Aguila Yanes; Nicolás Guillén Landrián; José Morales Rodríguez; Angel Tomás Quiñones González; Julio Soto Angurel; Francisco Tejera Garrido; and Eduardo Yanes Santana.

45. ECT is considered appropriate in cases of severe depression and catatonic schizophrenia. For a history of ECT as well as a description of its uses in modern psychiatry, see Richard D. Weiner, "Electroconvulsive Therapy," in Volume Two of Harold I. Kaplan and Benjamin J. Sudok, eds., *Comprehensive Textbook of Psychiatry, Fifth Edition* (Baltimore: Williams & Willkins, 1989), pp. 1670–1676 [hereafter cited as "Electroconvulsive Therapy"], and Barbara A. Weiner, "Treatment Rights," in S.J. Brakel, J. Parry, & B.A. Weiner, *The Mentally Disabled and the Law* (Chicago: American Bar Foundation, 1985), p. 330 [hereafter cited as "Treatment Rights"].

46. B.A. Weiner, "Treatment Rights," p. 330; R.D. Weiner, "Electroconvulsive Therapy," pp. 1671–2.

47. B.A. Weiner, "Treatment Rights," p. 330.

48. B.A. Weiner, "Treatment Rights," p. 331.

49. See the cases of José Luis Alvarado Delgado; Javier Roberto Bahamonde Masot; Eugenio de Sosa Chabau; Nicolás Guillén Landrián; Jesús Leyva Guerra; Orestes Martínez Haydar; Marcos Miranda Morales; Emilio Montero Romero; José Morales Rodríguez; and Julio Vento Roberes.

50. See the cases of Esteban Cárdenas Junquera; Eduardo Yanes Santana; and Andrés José Solares Teseiro.

51. See, for example, the case of Javier Roberto Bahamonde Masot.

52. As Richard Weiner notes in "Electroconvulsive Therapy" (p. 1671), there is some controversy within the psychiatric community as to whether a patient should be taken off of psychotropic drugs before being administered ECT. Regarding Cuba, there is no specific evidence that those being given ECT were under the influence of psychotropic drugs. However, the fact that a number of victims had psychotropic drugs mixed in with their food points to a conclusion that some patients were given ECT while under the influence of drugs.

53. José Morales Rodríguez who was held for eighteen days, received ECT, as did Julio Vento Roberes, who was held for five years.

54. See, for example, the case of Orestes Martínez Haydar.

55. See the cases of Eugenio de Sosa Chabau; Amaro Gómez Boix; Ariel Hidalgo Guillén; Eduardo Yanes Santana; Orestes Martínez Haydar; and Andrés José Solares Teseiro.

56. See the cases of Eugenio de Sosa Chabau and Orestes Martínez Haydar.

57. See the cases of Amaro Gómez Boix and Eduardo Yanes Santana.

58. In only one case was anesthesia given. Nicolás Guillén Landrián was forced to undergo a total of twenty sessions of ECT; twelve were under anesthesia. There is no record of any patient receiving muscle relaxants.

59. See, for example, the case of Amaro Gómez Boix, who has written that those administering the electroshocks often forgot to provide the rubber bit. As a result, when the electroshock was given, the victim's teeth "would grind down on his tongue, turning his mouth into a bloodied foam." See Amaro Gómez Boix, "Cuba: El *Electroshock* como arma politica, [Cuba: Electroshock as a Political Weapon]," part two of two in a series, *El Nuevo Herald (The Miami Herald),* 11 February 1989. The series is reprinted in the Appendix on pp. 139–145.

60. See the cases of Eugenio de Sosa Chabau; Jesús Leyva Guerra; and Orestes Martínez Haydar.

61. See the cases of Amaro Gómez Boix and Orestes Martínez Haydar.

62. See the case of Eugenio de Sosa Chabau.

63. As mentioned above, Esteban Cárdenas Junquera, Eduardo Yanes Santana, and Andrés José Solares Teseiro all were forced to watch.

64. See the cases of Eugenio de Sosa Chabau and Eduardo Yanes Santana.

65. See, for example, the cases of Javier Roberto Bahamonde Masot and Jesús Leyva Guerra.

66. See B.A. Weiner, "Treatment Rights," p. 329.

67. *The Physicians' Desk Reference* (Oradell, New Jersey: Medical Economics Company, 1989) p. 2071.

68. According to Volume II of *Advice for the Patient: Drug Information in Lay Language,* phenothiazines "are used to treat nervous, mental, and emotional conditions. Some are used also to control anxiety in certain patients" (Rockville, Maryland: United States Pharmacopeial Convention, 1989), p. 974. According to the 1989 edition of *The Physicians Desk Reference* (p. 2071), phenothiazines such as chlorpromazine are used "for the management of manifestations of psychotic disorders. . . [and] to control the manifestations of the manic type of manic depressive illness."

69. *The Physicians' Desk Reference,* p. 2073.

70. *The Physicians Desk Reference,* p. 2073.

71. For a complete list of the side effects of phenothiazines, see *Advice for the Patient,* pp. 976–977.

72. *The Physicians Desk Reference,* p. 2071.

73. *The Physicians Desk Reference* (p. 2071) states that "the likelihood that [tardic dyskinesia] will become irreversible [is] believed to increase as the duration of treatment and the total cumulative dose. . . increase."

74. *The Physicians' Desk Reference,* pp. 2072–2073.

75. To quote *The Physicians' Desk Reference,* "[g]iven the likelihood that some patients exposed chronically to [phenothiazines] will develop tardive dyskinesia, it is advised that all patients in whom chronic use is contemplated be given, if possible, full information about this risk. The decision to inform patients and/or their guardians must obviously take into account the clinical circumstances and the competency of the patient to understand the information provided" (p. 2071). According to B.A. Weiner in "Treatment Rights," the question of whether patients should have the right to refuse treatment with psychotropic drugs is "the most controversial area of litigation in mental health today. . . . Some courts and some legislatures have already recognized this right. The controversy is likely to continue at least until treatments having no side effects can be developed for the mentally ill" (p. 330). See also Michael L. Perlin, "Patients' Rights," in G.H. Klerman, et. al., *Psychiatry,* Volume Five: *Social, Epidemiological and Legal Psychiatry* (Philadelphia: J.B. Lippincott, 1986), pp. 405–408 [hereafter cited as "Patients' Rights"].

76. See *The Physicians' Desk Reference,* p. 2071; and *Advice for the Patient,* p. 2073.

77. See the cases of Silvio Aguila Yanes; José Luis Alvarado Delgado; Javier Roberto Bahamonde Masot; Esteban Cárdenas Junquera; Eugenio de Sosa Chabau; Juan Manuel García Cao; Amaro Gómez Boix; Nicolás Guillén Landrián; Gualdo Hidalgo Portilla; Jesús Leyva Guerra; Orestes Martínez Haydar; José Morales Rodríguez; Julio Vento Roberes; Eduardo Yanes Santana; and F. Mario Zaldívar Batista.

78. See, for example, the case of José Luis Alvarado Delgado..

79. See, for example, the case of Eugenio DeSosa Chabau.

80. See the cases of Esteban Cárdenas Junquera and Amaro Gómez Boix.

81. See, for example, the cases of José Luis Alvarado Delgado and Jesús Leyva Guerra.

82. The following section is based in large part upon B.A. Weiner, "Treatment Rights," pp. 327–351; and Perlin, "Patients' Rights," pp. 401–422.

83. Fundamental to the right to treatment is the concept that when the state confines an individual to an institution, it is "legally, morally and ethically compelled to treat the person as well." Perlin, "Patients' Rights," p. 402. See also B.A. Weiner, "Treatment Rights," p. 334.

84. See, for example, the ruling of the United States Supreme Court in 1972 that "the nature and duration of commitment [must] bear a reasonable relationship to the purpose for which the individual is committed." Quoted in Perlin, "Patients' Rights," p. 401.

85. Perlin, "Patients' Rights," p. 402.

86. As noted earlier, the right to refuse treatment is not universally accepted. See Perlin, "Patients' Rights," pp. 405–408; B.A. Weiner, "Treatment Rights," pp. 341–351.

87. The International Covenant on Civil and Political Rights states that "no one shall be subjected without his free consent to medical or scientific experimentation." See the International Covenant on Civil and Political Rights, Part III, Article Seven, as reprinted in United Nations, Centre for Human Rights, *Human Rights: A Compilation of International Instruments* (New York: United Nations Publications, 1988), p. 21.

88. Perlin, "Patients' Rights," p. 402.

89. Perlin, "Patients' Rights," pp. 402–403.

90. See, for example the cases of Orestes Martínez Haydar, who was given electroshocks after refusing to ingest psychotropic drugs, and Emilio Montero Romero, who was confined to a punishment cell in the Castellanos ward of the Havana Psychiatric Hospital (Mazorra) after he objected to being given electroshock therapy.

91. See the cases of Javier Roberto Bahamonde Masot and Juan Manuel García Cao.

92. The Convention against Torture is reprinted in *Human Rights: A Compilation of International Instruments,* pp. 212–226.

93. A record of Cuba's adherence to the Convention can be found in United Nations, Centre for Human Rights, *Human Rights: Status of International Instruments* (New York: United Nations Publications, 1988), p. 228. There is no record of any possible reservations Cuba may have made at the time of its signing.

94. International Convention against Tortu.e and Other Cruel, Inhuman or Degrading Treatment or Punishment, Part I, Article 1, Section 1, as reprinted in *A Compilation of International Instruments,* p. 213.

95. Amnesty International, *Torture in the Eighties: An Amnesty International Report* (London: Amnesty International, 1984), p. 4.

96. Amnesty International, *Torture in the Eighties: An Amnesty International Report,* pp. 13–14.

97. Elena O. Nightingale, "The Problem of Torture and the Response of the Health Professional," in Janet Gruschow and Kari Hannibal, eds., *Health Services for the Treatment of Torture and Trauma Survivors* (Washington: American Association for the Advancement of Science, Directorate for Science and Policy Programs, 1990), pp. 8–9.

II
CASE HISTORIES

THE TEENAGER

Born in Havana on 10 June 1964, José Luis Alvarado Delgado attended Enrique Masa and Manolito Aguiar Workers' Pre-University High Schools in Havana. On 22 November 1980, the sixteen year-old Alvarado sought political asylum at the Colombian Embassy in Havana. A Cuban guard at the Embassy arrested Alvarado and turned him over to State Security agents, who took him to their headquarters at *Villa Marista* in Havana. He was held in a small, cold cell, and interrogated continually for one week. His interrogators threatened to send him to the Havana Psychiatric Hospital (Mazorra), warning that violently insane patients would rape and beat him.

JOSÉ ALVARADO DELGADO
OCCUPATION: STUDENT
DIAGNOSIS: SANE
CONFINEMENT: 1 MONTH
ELECTROSHOCKS: 3
PSYCHOTROPIC DRUGS: YES

When Alvarado refused to cooperate, he was transferred to the Carbó-Serviá ward of the Havana Psychiatric Hospital (Mazorra). At their first meeting, his psychiatrist spent more time asking him about his detention than his mental health. Their second meeting consisted of a battery of exams, including an encephalograph and an intelligence test. During their third meeting, the psychiatrist told him

> that I did not have any psychiatric problems and that State Security had taken me [to Carbó-Serviá] because I had not wanted to sign a self-incriminating confession. "But you knew these things already," she said. "If you do not cooperate, it will be worse for you."

Later that same day, an orderly and one of his inmate trusties seized Alvarado, placed a rubber bit in his mouth, and forced

45

him to undergo electroconvulsive therapy until he became unconscious. When he regained consciousness, he discovered that the shocks had caused him to lose control of his bowels. When he protested, members of the hospital staff held him down and force fed him psychotropic drugs. From that day on,

> I was forced to take psychotropic drugs three times daily. . . The reaction was immediate. You felt like everything around you slowly was losing its animation. You felt far away. You could walk, eat, and talk, but they were involuntary reflexes. The moment would come when you could not remember anything — neither your name nor that of the friend beside you. It was like being awake and dreaming at the same time. The real was confused with the unreal.

Alvarado later told Don Schanche of *The Los Angeles Times,* "They used the psychiatric hospital to destroy the will of the person."

When he continued to refuse to sign a self-incriminating confession, a State Security agent warned him that "whether you want to or not, sooner or later you will give in." Enraged, Alvarado struck the agent. Several inmate trusties seized him and, following the orders of one of the doctors, took him to the punishment cells of the Castellanos ward. At odd hours of the day and night, one of the orderlies or one of the inmate trusties would spray the prisoners with water. Alvarado was forced to undergo a second session of electroshock therapy, and force fed additional large doses of psychotropic drugs. After three days in Castellanos (and a total of three weeks in Mazorra), Alvarado concluded that if he did not sign a confession, he "would be totally destroyed." Upon signing, he was sentenced to one year in jail, which he served at the Combinado del Este Prison in Havana. He was released on 22 November 1981, one year to the day after he had sought asylum.

On 22 March 1982, Alvarado was arrested while trying to send photos that he claimed would document Cuba's training of Latin American subversive groups to the United States Interest Section in Havana. Once again he refused to cooperate with State Security or sign a confession. After a brief detention in *Villa Marista*, he was returned to Carbó-Serviá, where during a one week stay he was subjected to a third series of electroshocks and large doses of psychotropic drugs. By the time he was returned to *Villa Marista*, he had lost part of his memory, and could not control his automatic reflexes. Alvarado later said that he was so disoriented that when the authorities handed him a confession, he signed it. He was sentenced to six years in prison. For one week he was held in solitary confinement in the maximum security wing of La Cabaña Prison. He later was transferred to the Combinado del Este Prison in Havana. On 30 May 1986, he was released on parole.

On 25 June 1986, Alvarado gave an interview to a Reuters correspondent in Havana. He spoke about his own experiences and denounced the incarceration of other political prisoners. In late August, he was arrested and accused of breaking the conditions of his parole. Authorities alleged that he had tried to obtain a visa from the United States and had tried to obtain asylum in the Venezuelan Embassy. He was sentenced to an additional year in prison, and was ordered to serve the last two years of his earlier sentence. Alvarado spent the next eighteen months in solitary confinement in the infamous "Rectangle of Death" maximum security ward of Combinado del Este Prison. He was released on 19 March 1988.

In October 1988, he was arrested and detained for two days for complaining that the Cuban government would not give him an exit visa. On 20 March 1989, he was arrested and detained briefly while trying to make arrangements at the Swiss Embassy for his departure from Cuba. He finally managed to leave Cuba for Europe on 9 April 1989.

SOURCES

Amnesty International, "Urgent Action" News Release, 25 September 1986, p. 1.

Amnesty International, *Cuba: Political Imprisonment, An Update* (London: Amnesty International, January 1988), p. 3.

Amnesty International, *Cuba: Recent Developments Affecting the Situation of Political Prisoners and the Use of the Death Penalty* (London: Amnesty International, September 1988), p. 29.

Mary Jane Camejo, *Human Rights in Cuba: The Need to Maintain the Pressure* (New York: Americas Watch, January 1989), pp. 12, 27, 99–100.

Don A. Schanche, "Cuban Rights Crackdown, Psychiatric Abuses Told," *The Los Angeles Times,* 28 January 1989.

Written Statement, 9 May 1990.

THE DEFECTOR

Born in La Lisa, Havana province on 4 May 1962, **Silvio Aguila Yanes** graduated from his local municipal high school.

SILVIO AGUILA YANES
OCCUPATION: STUDENT
DIAGNOSIS: UNKNOWN
CONFINEMENT: ONE WEEK
ELECTROSHOCKS: 4
PSYCHOTROPIC DRUGS: YES

On 7 June 1980, Silvio and his brother Sergio were among a group who attempted to flee Cuba by hijacking a boat used on the Canímar River to Varadero Beach run in Matanzas province. Although they managed to take control of the boat, the hijackers almost immediately began to be pursued by craft from both the Cuban Navy and State Security. The hijacked boat was fired upon and sunk in Cuban waters. Ten died. In the turmoil surrounding the sinking boat, Silvio managed to save a woman and her child from drowning. Sergio, who was a member of the Cuban armed forces at the time of the hijacking, was pulled from the water by Cuban Naval personnel; he has not been seen since, and is feared dead.

Silvio was taken to the Havana Psychiatric Hospital (Mazorra) and confined to the Castellanos and Carbó-Serviá wards for one week. In Carbó-Serviá, he was given four electroshocks under the supervision of Heriberto Mederos, an orderly who allegedly works for the Ministry of the Interior. He also was forced to ingest psychotropic drugs.

In a highly publicized trial, the Cuban government requested that Silvio be given the death penalty for his part in the hijacking. He was found guilty and sentenced to thirty years in prison. Although he was held for a brief time in La Cabaña Prison, he almost immediately was transferred to Combinado del Este Prison in Havana. He spent his first two years there in the infamous "Rectangle of Death" punishment ward. He later was transferred to Building Number Three (South Wing, Fourth

Floor, Cell 52), where he refused to participate in a re-education program and became one of the *nuevos plantados.*[1]

Silvio Aguila reportedly has been the victim of several beatings at the hands of Cuban prison officials—beatings which allegedly have endangered his life. On 8 December 1988, after he was beaten savagely, he managed to smuggle out of prison a message written in blood on a pair of underwear.

Although he has not yet been released from prison, he has applied for a visa to emigrate to the United States. The U.S. Immigration and Naturalization Service reportedly has refused his visa application on the basis of his role in the hijacking.

SOURCES

Affidavit, Julio Vento Roberes, 18 October 1990. (Vento was confined with Aguila in the Havana Psychiatric Hospital (Mazorra) and later in Combinado del Este prison.)

"Sumario del 17 de Enero de 1989, [Summary of 17 January 1989]," in Ricardo Bofill, editor, *Resumen del Informe Anual de 1989 sobre la Situación de los Derechos Humanos en Cuba* [*Summary of the 1989 Annual Report on the Situation of Human Rights in Cuba*] (Miami: Comité Cubano Pro Derechos Humanos, 1989), p. 2

---

[1]*Plantados* are Cuban political prisoners who refuse to undergo the standard "rehabiliation and re-education" program that, among other things, requires participants to wear the blue uniform of the common prisoners. The original group of *plantados* were imprisoned in the early and mid-1960s. The group known as *nuevos plantados* were imprisoned in the late 1970s and early 1980s.

THE CANDIDATE

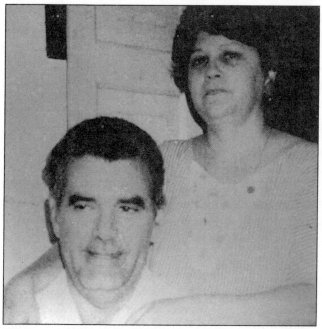

Roberto and Rafaela Bahamonde at home in Havana, Cuba (1989)
[Photo: George Gedda]

J. ROBERTO BAHAMONDE MASOT
OCCUPATION: AGRICULTURAL ENGINEER
DIAGNOSIS: PARANOIA
CONFINEMENT: 40 DAYS
ELECTROSHOCKS: 8
PSYCHOTROPIC DRUGS: YES

Born in Matanzas on 3 December 1935, **Javier Roberto Bahamonde Masot** graduated from the University of Havana with degrees in education and agricultural engineering. First arrested on 26 June 1971 for writing Cuban President Fidel Castro to suggest increasing production through material incentives, he was taken to State Security Headquarters at *Villa Marista* in Havana for fifteen days of interrogation. He was confined for four days at the Havana Psychiatric Hospital

51

(Mazorra). Upon his release, he was given a document stating that he had been diagnosed as paranoid.

On 27 May 1975, Bahamonde was arrested while working as an agronomist at the Bacuranao State Dairy Farm in Campo Florido, Havana province. He was taken to State Security Headquarters at *Villa Marista* in Havana, where he was interrogated for twenty days. According to Amnesty International, Cuban authorities accused him of "having written a document of a counter-revolutionary nature and. . . having devoted himself to formulating repeated and systematic expressions of this nature, as well [as] carrying out proselytizing work of the same kind." On 1 July, the Court of Crimes against State Security determined that Bahamonde was "in a state of dangerousness," and committed him to the Carbó-Serviá ward of the Havana Psychiatric Hospital (Mazorra). For the next three weeks, he witnessed a variety of horrors: regular beatings; ranting, criminally insane inmates wandering the ward naked; walls and floors covered with urine, vomit and excrement; and the abuse of electroconvulsive therapy (ECT) under the supervision of the orderly Heriberto Mederos. Bahamonde was forced to undergo eight sessions of ECT and ingest large doses of psychotropic drugs. He since has stated that none of the hospital's psychiatrists authorized or attended these sessions. In a 1989 interview with George Gedda of the Associated Press, Bahamonde said that as a result of ECT, he suffered hypersensitivity and significant memory loss:

> It took me years to recover. I recognized my family, but there were friends whose names I did not remember. . . . You lose your memory. You can't even remember people's names. I thought I would even forget what I learned in the university. . . . But little by little, I got my memory back. I think now I'm all right. I feel good.

On 22 July 1975, he was transferred to prison.[1] He was released in March 1976.

In 1980, Bahamonde was fired from his job as an agronomist and had to survive by doing odd jobs. In 1983, he began working as a freelance photographer. Cuban authorities refused to issue him the license required by law for those who are self-employed. In January 1983, he was arrested and falsely accused of plotting to murder Castro. On 19 January 1983, he was committed to Carbó-Serviá for fifteen days. On 11 February, he was transferred to *Villa Marista*. After a total of fifty-six days in *Villa Marista* and Carbó-Serviá, he was released.

While Bahamonde was in Carbó-Serviá, his wife Rafaela came to visit him. As she later explained, she was horrified by what she found: "I felt like throwing up. I had to see him there amid all the stench." When she complained about ward conditions to the office of Eduardo Bernabé Ordaz Ducungé, M.D., the hospital's director, she was told that Ordaz had no authority over Carbó-Serviá, as it fell under the jurisdiction of the Ministry of the Interior.

Upon his release, Bahamonde again worked as a free-lance photographer and joined the Cuban Commission on Human Rights and National Reconciliation (*Comisión Cubana de Derechos Humanos y Reconciliación Nacional*, or CCDHRN) and the Cuban Human Rights Party (*Partido Pro Derechos Humanos de Cuba*). On 20 September 1988, he was arrested outside the Comodoro Hotel while trying to testify before a delegation of the United Nations Commission on Human Rights then visiting Cuba. After being held for four hours at a police station in Miramar, a suburb of Havana, he was released.

---

[1] The authors could not determine to which prison Bahamonde was sent. Several sources, including George Gedda of The Associated Press and Adela Bahamonde Cervantes (his sister), claim that Bahamonde was held in the Havana Psychiatric Hospital for ten months.

On 20 March 1989, Bahamonde ran for a municipal assembly seat from his district in San Miguel de Padron, a section of Havana. Despite the fact that Cuban authorities prevented him from presenting his platform, Bahamonde managed to tally thirty-one of ninety-one votes cast. Fifty-nine voters abstained. Bahamonde since has stated that he believes that those who abstained sympathized with his views but feared supporting him openly. On 4 April 1989, Bahamonde was arrested and charged with illegal association and participation in an illegal demonstration. At his closed trial three days later, he was denied benefit of counsel and sentenced to three months for "illicit meetings" with foreign reporters. It appears that Bahamonde's arrest and conviction had as much to do with the plans of the CCDHRN to hold a demonstration outside the Soviet Embassy during the visit of Soviet President Mikhail Gorbachev as they did with his candidacy. On 9 June 1989, while in Combinado del Sur Prison in Matanzas province, he was tried in absentia, found guilty of taking photos without a license under Article 228 of the Cuban Criminal Code, and sentenced to an additional year in prison. He was released on 2 July 1990.

SOURCES

Americas Watch, *Cuba: Jailing the Human Rights Movement* (New York: Americas Watch, 1990), p. 10.

Americas Watch, *Human Rights Activists behind Bars in Cuba* (New York: Americas Watch, 1989), p. 4.

Amnesty International, *Cuba: Arrest and Imprisonment of Human Rights Party Members* (London: Amnesty International, June 1989), pp. 6–7.

Amnesty International, *Cuba: Political Imprisonment, A Summary of Recent Concerns* (London: Amnesty International, 1989), p. 10.

George Gedda, "Testing Cuba's Limits: One Dissident's Quest for Free Expression," *Foreign Service Journal* (May 1990): 24–28.

George Gedda, "Cuba: Dissident, Office Seeker, Free Market Advocate, Loses in Rare Cuban Election," Associated Press wire story, 6 April 1990.

Havana Psychiatric Hospital, certificate of discharge in case of Javier Roberto Bahamonde Masot, 21 January 1983.

Interview, Mrs. Adela Bahamonde Cervantes (sister), 17 April 1990.

Judgement of 24 July 1975, Court of Crimes against the Security of the State, Havana, Cuba, Judgement number 177/75, Case number 25/75.G

THE REFUSENIK

ESTEBAN CÁRDENAS JUNQUERA
OCCUPATION: EDUCATOR
DIAGNOSIS: PSYCHOTIC
CONFINEMENT: 24 DAYS
ELECTROSHOCKS: NONE
PSYCHOTROPIC DRUGS: YES

Born 16 July 1946 in Ciego de Avila, Camagüey province, Esteban Cárdenas Junquera graduated from Manuel Azcunce High School in Tarará, Havana province, in 1963. In 1966, after three years in the School of Education at the University of Havana, he was expelled for "anti-Soviet attitudes." In March 1970, he was arrested for refusing to serve in the Cuban Armed Forces and detained in Morro Castle Prison in Havana. In May, he was transferred to the Castellanos ward of the Havana Psychiatric Hospital (Mazorra), where doctors diagnosed him as a "psychotic personality with the ability to differentiate between right and wrong." During his three-week stay, he was given five hundred milligrams of chlorpromazine on a daily basis and was forced to watch while electroshocks were administered to other dissidents. Cárdenas later said that he believes the purpose of his internment was not to cure but to frighten and demoralize him. He since has described the inhuman living conditions in Castellanos. Human excrement covered the floor. He shared two towels and one bar of soap with nineteen criminally insane inmates. Under the supervision of the orderly Heriberto Mederos, two inmate trusties named "Mayarí" and "Caballo" conducted a reign of terror.[1] After twenty-four days in Castellanos, Cárdenas

---

[1]*Mayarí* is a town in central Cuba; *caballo* literally means "horse."

56

was returned to Morro Castle, tried, and sentenced to six months forced labor on a crew assigned to Havana's Metropolitan Park Program. After his release, Cárdenas began to work as a temporary at the Center for Information and Study of Culture. In May 1971, he was arrested and charged with vagrancy. Because his name was not on the Center's official payroll, he was found guilty and sentenced to one year in prison. After serving his term at El Príncipe Prison and performing forced labor on a dairy farm in San José de las Lajas, he won his appeal and was released. In 1972, he worked for *Bohemia* magazine for nine months until he was fired for "ideological deviationism." In 1974, he worked as an advisor on literature to rural schools in Jagüey Grande, Matanzas province, until he again was fired for "deviationism." From 1975 until his arrest in 1978, he worked in the Publications Department of the National Library in Havana. In March 1977, he was detained for seventy-two hours at State Security Headquarters at *Villa Marista* for his allegedly "revisionist" writings. On 2 September 1977, he was arrested and detained for three hours at *Villa Marista* in Havana. Although he was accused of plotting to leave Cuba illegally and kidnapping a government official, he was released. On 21 March 1978, Cárdenas sought asylum in the Argentinean Embassy by jumping into its garden from an adjoining roof. He broke his ankle during the attempt. The Embassy called the police. State Security agents arrested him and carried him from the Embassy grounds. He was sentenced to fifteen years in prison, of which he served twenty months. Released on 13 October 1979, he came to the United States in January 1980. He currently resides in Miami, Florida.

SOURCES

Afffidavit, 6 December 1990.

Nestor Almendros & Jorge Ulla, *Nobody Listened* (New York: Cuban Human Rights Project, 1988), Film.

THE BUSINESSMAN

EUGENIO DE SOSA CHABAU
OCCUPATION: BUSINESS EXECUTIVE
DIAGNOSIS: NONE
CONFINEMENT: 5 MONTHS
ELECTROSHOCKS: 14
PSYCHOTROPIC DRUGS: YES

Born in Havana on 8 August 1916, **Eugenio de Sosa Chabau** attended schools in Cuba, the United States, Great Britain, and Switzerland, and studied diplomatic and consular law at the University of Havana. He was a member of the Board of Directors of the daily newspaper *Diario de la Marina*, and presided over the Santa Regina Sugar Mill as well as cattle ranch operations. In December 1959, he was arrested for conspiring to depose the Castro regime and was sentenced to twenty years in jail and an additional twenty years under house arrest. Over the following years, he was confined to several prisons, including the Isle of Pines and La Cabaña. He was one of the *plantados*, prisoners who refused to participate in reeducation programs or wear the uniform of common prisoners.

In 1977, after seventeen years in prison, de Sosa was taken from Combinado del Este Prison to State Security Headquarters at *Villa Marista* to be interrogated on information he allegedly passed to "counter-revolutionary exiles" in 1963. He was stripped and placed in solitary confinement in a small, unlit cell. Psychotropic drugs were mixed in with his food; when he discovered a half-dissolved tablet in his food, he stopped eating.

One day, he was interrogated by a State Security officer, who told him that one of his daughters (whom he had not seen in over fifteen years) and his granddaughters were flying in from Texas to visit him. The officer told him that the visit was "a gesture of mercy of the Castro government" before his execution. A few days later, de Sosa was taken to the barber and given clean clothes. When he entered the room, however, he found not his family but the same State Security officer, who told him that there had been a terrible accident involving the plane, and that his daughter and granddaughters were dead. (De Sosa later discovered that both the visit and the death of his family were a hoax.) Enraged, he struck the State Security officer. As de Sosa later put it, "when I was told of the 'tragedy,' I believed it. . . . I wanted to die." The guards beat him savagely, telling him he would be shot the next day at La Cabaña Prison.

That night, however, he instead was taken from *Villa Marista* and driven through Havana. At one point, he was forced to lie down on the floor of the car. When he was removed from the car, he discovered that he had been transferred to the Carbó-Serviá ward of the Havana Psychiatric Hospital (Mazorra). De Sosa later described Carbó-Serviá as "a snakepit writhing with the violent and insane."

> There were about eighty men in this ward, all violently disturbed. The smell of urine and excrement was sickening. There would be brawls among the patients every so often and shattered, bloody bodies had to be carted out. During my stay there, five patients were killed in brawls. . . .

One day, several young boys, the oldest of whom probably was no more than 16, were brought into the ward:

> [The boys] had been caught writing anti-government graffiti on some building walls, and a "judge of the people" declared that to do such a thing they must be insane and in need of psychiatric treatment. Before the day was over all the boys were systematically gang-raped by more that thirty patients in the ward. To this day I can hear their cries for

59

help and see their bloody bodies as I stood by in impotent rage. Not a single staff member intervened.

During his time in Carbó-Serviá, de Sosa was subjected to fourteen sessions of electroconvulsive therapy. As he later described, most electroshocks were applied with little or no regard for the health or safety of the patient:

My first encounter with group electroshock treatments occurred one night when I saw a team of four men, directed by a man called Mederos who was dressed as an orderly, enter the ward. Six patients were grabbed and rubber pieces stuffed into their mouths. They were thrown to the floor in a row side by side. Right there, on the floor, the electrodes were applied to both sides of their heads and the shocks [were] applied. Six bodies started to contort one by one. . . . The shocks were applied to the temples of the patients, but to me they applied most of the shocks to the testicles instead.

He later told Lourdes Meluza of WLTV-TV in Miami that electroshocks "felt like thunder, an explosion."

After five months, he was returned to Combinado del Este, where he remained until his release on 15 November 1979. He arrived in the United States on 18 January 1980. He now is an independent associate with the Calmaquip Engineering Corporation in Miami, Florida.

SOURCES

Affidavit, 10 July 1990.

Eugenio de Sosa, "A Witness to Cuban Tyranny," *The New York Post*, 1 November 1984.

Eugenio de Sosa, "The Interrogation," from *In a Place without a Soul: The Testimony of Former Cuban Political Prisoners* (Washington: United States Information Agency, March 1985).

Eugenio de Sosa, Interview with Lourdes Meluza, 1990. Part of "Psychiatric Abuse in Cuba," a news series by WLTV-TV, Miami.

THE STUDENT

JUAN MANUEL GARCÍA CAO
OCCUPATION: STUDENT
DIAGNOSIS: SANE
CONFINEMENT: 2 DAYS
ELECTROSHOCKS: NO
PSYCHOTROPIC DRUGS: YES

Born in Havana on 8 July 1961, **Juan Manuel García Cao** graduated from Pablo de la Torriente Brau High School in Havana. In 1979, he began to study cinematography at the National Film Institute (*Instituto Cubano de Arte e Industria Cinematográfica*, or ICAIC). On 30 January 1982, he was dismissed from school, arrested, and accused of contempt for the regime and writing subversive literature. He was taken to State Security Headquarters at *Villa Marista* in Havana, and spent the next seventeen days under interrogation.

On 16 February 1982, García Cao was transferred to the Carbó-Serviá ward of the Havana Psychiatric Hospital (Mazorra). He remembers his two days confined with the criminally insane inmates of Carbó-Serviá as the worst of his three years in prison:

> It was like Dante's *Inferno*. Fights broke out among the inmates continually. Some detainees were raped. The patients were sedated, as heavy doses of tranquilizers were mixed in with the food.

After a battery of tests, the attending psychiatrist asked García Cao why he had been brought to the hospital because it was clear that he was sane. Despite this admission, he was not released. García Cao since has stated that a Dr. Fleitas was in charge of the ward, and that the events he witnessed were done

62

with Fleitas' complicity. At no time during his stay in Carbó-Serviá did his family know that he was confined there. They found out only when Adriana Chavez Solares, the wife of Andrés Solares, another dissident detained in Carbó-Serviá, told them that her husband had seen García Cao.

After two days, he was transferred to Combinado del Este Prison in Havana, where he was held for one month. He was sentenced to three years in prison for writing "enemy propaganda against the revolution" and confined to La Cabaña Prison. He spent the next eight months confined to a ward with common prisoners. He eventually was moved to Building Number One of Combinado del Este, where he spent eleven months confined with common criminals. He was released in October 1984, two months before his sentence was due to expire.

Upon his release, García Cao worked for eight months in a print shop. He then performed odd jobs until he received an exit visa. He departed for Panama on 11 June 1986, and emigrated to the United States on 11 September 1988. He currently is a producer for *Univision* Channel 23 in Miami, and recently won a local Emmy award for a campaign promoting Channel 23 News. He writes a bimonthly column for *El Nuevo Herald*, the Spanish language supplement of *The Miami Herald*.

SOURCES

Affidavit, 1 July 1990.

Interview with Andrés Solares Teseiro, 6 June 1990.

Telephone Interview, 8 June 1990.

THE JOURNALIST

AMARO GÓMEZ BOIX
OCCUPATION: JOURNALIST
DIAGNOSIS: SANE
CONFINEMENT: 14 DAYS
ELECTROSHOCKS: NONE
PSYCHOTROPIC DRUGS: YES

Born in 1935 in Santiago de Cuba, **Amaro Gómez Boix** attended Candler College and Trelles High Schools in Havana. Upon graduation, he became a scriptwriter for the National Film Institute (ICAIC). In 1964, he resigned as a result of his dissidence from the Castro regime and started to write clandestinely. In 1965 he wrote training manuals for the state-owned Havana Construction and Mining Companies. In 1966, he worked at *Instituto Cubano de Radio y Televisión* (ICRT) as a writer for "Weekly Review", which aired every Sunday on *Radio Reloj*. In the aftermath of the 1971 Padilla Affair,[1] he was fired and declared a dissident.

From 1971 to 1978, he worked in a shoe factory, continuing to write on the side. In 1978, State Security agents searched his home in the Vedado section of Havana for nine hours. They found ten unpublished book-length manuscripts written by Gómez, a copy of Aleksandr Solzhenitsyn's *Gulag Archipelago*, and an anti-Castro leaflet written in verse. He was taken to State Security Headquarters at *Villa Marista* and held for thirty-five days. One day, a guard entered his cell and told Gómez to follow him. He was taken to a room where he found the clothes he

---

[1] The "Padilla Affair" refers to the 1971 imprisonment and "confession" of the poet Herberto Padilla. The event was used by the Castro regime to mount a purge against "intellectuals." Castro charged that Jean Paul Sartre, Simone de Beauvior, Susan Sontag, and others who protested Padilla's imprisonment were agents of the Central Intelligence Agency (CIA).

64

had been wearing when he was arrested. After he dressed, the guard escorted him to a door at the rear of the building, handcuffed him, and put him in the back seat of a car. Gómez was told by the guard that he was being taken to the Havana Psychiatric Hospital (Mazorra), where he would be given a thorough psychiatric examination. Upon his arrival, he was taken to an office, where "a rather calm-looking policeman disguised as a doctor" examined Gómez's testicles, wrote something down on a pad of paper, and asked Gómez for his toothbrush. When Gómez gave it to him, he snapped off the handle of the toothbrush, threw the handle away, and returned the rest to Gómez.

Gómez then was escorted to "a section of the hospital where the doors had bars," which he later found out was known as the Carbó-Serviá ward. He was told to undress, handed a bar of soap and a towel, and ordered to shower. He was issued a uniform and taken to a courtyard, which he later found out was known among the inmates as *La Perrera* (the Dog Kennel). Bordered on one side by the hospital, *La Perrera* was surrounded by three fifteen to twenty feet-high concrete walls. In place of a roof, there was a latticework of iron bars with two wooden planks at the center; on the planks stood a sentry with an automatic rifle.

Each evening, before dinner, the inmates lined up, their mouths open and tongues extended, waiting for an orderly to come by and place a dose of thorazine on each tongue. Almost every morning, a man named Mederos would enter the ward. Nicknamed *El Enfermero* (the Nurse) by the inmates, Mederos is described by Gómez as "a short, somewhat paunchy man who dresses in civilian clothes and a small, short-brimmed hat."[2] Mederos gave electroshocks to a variety of internees, including some political prisoners:

---

[2]This probably is Heriberto Mederos, named by others as the man who gave them ECT. However, Gómez does not remember his first name.

Amaro Gómez Boix and his daughter, Oday Gómez Mesa (1990).

Almost every day, his various assistants call out loudly the names of the unfortunate chosen who will be asked to lie down on the wet cement so that the electrical current will travel better. Mederos then fastens the electrodes and the entire process is performed routinely, which often entails overlooking the placement of a rubber bit in the prisoner's mouth. It is no surprise then, that when that first jolt of power zaps the prisoner's body, his teeth grind down on his tongue, turning his mouth into a bloodied foam.

Gómez never underwent electroconvulsive therapy; the authorities seemed to believe that seeing others suffer would intimidate him into cooperating. Gómez also tells of a man called *El Capitán* (the Captain) by the inmates:

> Then there's *El Capitán*, the chief of the wing, who sodomizes the younger prisoners, threatening to turn them over

66

to his two deranged bodyguards or to Mederos if they don't cooperate. . . . I can remember that after being raped, one young prisoner—who couldn't have been more than fourteen or fifteen years old—spent hours upon hours staring blankly, aimlessly into space, without ever really seeing. "It was *El Capitán*," I was told by a veteran.

After two weeks, Gómez was taken from Carbó-Serviá and interviewed by a young man who worked for State Security. He warned Gómez to cooperate:

You've seen that the conditions here are not the best. It wouldn't be very good for you if you had to come back here. You've really got to have a lot of courage to return here, Amaro.

Roughly forty-eight hours later, the man returned. Despite the fact that he had continued to refuse to cooperate, Gómez (to his surprise) was not returned to the hospital, but was transferred to Combinado del Este Prison, where he spent the next eighteen months. After he was released in a 1979 amnesty, Gómez emigrated to Miami, Florida. Since 1980, he has worked as a news writer and editor for *Univision*, the Spanish-language television network, as well as other broadcasting firms in the United States.

SOURCES

Affidavit, 6 November 1990.

Amaro Gómez Boix, "Persistencia de la oscuridad (The Persistence of Darkness)," *El Nuevo Herald (The Miami Herald)*, 10 February 1989.

Amaro Gómez Boix, "Cuba: El *Electroshock* como arma política (Cuba: Electroshock as a Political Weapon)," *El Nuevo Herald (The Miami Herald)*, 11 February 1989.

Interview, 11 March 1990.

THE FILMMAKER

NICOLÁS GUILLÉN LANDRIÁN
OCCUPATION: FILMMAKER/ARTIST
DIAGNOSIS: UNKNOWN
CONFINEMENT: 5 YEARS
ELECTROSHOCKS: 20
PSYCHOTROPIC DRUGS: YES

A filmmaker, artist and poet, **Nicolás Guillén Landrián** was born in 1938 in Camagüey. He is the nephew of Cuba's late poet laureate, Nicolás Guillén. He graduated from Escuelas Pías High School and enrolled in the University of Havana, where he participated in the Revolution. In 1962, Cuban authorities accused him of trying to leave Cuba without authorization and sentenced him to two years at a "rehabilitation farm" on the Isle of Pines. After a year, he developed a nervous disorder and was allowed to complete his sentence under house arrest, but not before being confined for a brief time in the Galigarcía Hospital (later known as Centro de Salud Mental) in Havana, where he underwent twelve sessions of electroconvulsive therapy (ECT) under anesthesia.

In 1970, Guillén was arrested and detained briefly in Combinado del Este Prison in Havana. In 1973, the National Film Institute (ICAIC) expelled him for films "inconsistent with the goals of the revolution." ICAIC authorities had discovered that his documentary, *Coffea Arábiga* (*Arabian Coffee*), contained a scene showing Fidel Castro climbing a

68

mountain while the Beatles' song, *Fool on the Hill,* played in the background. Another factor in his expulsion was his refusal to participate in a film intended to discredit the poet Heberto Padilla. Unable to make a living as a filmmaker, he did odd jobs in the construction industry. In 1976, Guillén was accused of "ideological deviationism" and of conspiring to assassinate Fidel Castro. The latter charge apparently was based on an offhand remark made at a party. Taken to State Security Headquarters at *Villa Marista* in Havana, he was held without trial and interrogated for six months. In 1977, he was sentenced to two years in Combinado del Este Prison. Confined to the psychiatric unit of the Combinado del Este Prison hospital, he was given large doses of psychotropic drugs. His health broken, he was sent on the recommendation of State Security to the Carbó-Serviá ward of the Havana Psychiatric Hospital (Mazorra), where the orderly Heriberto Mederos supervised the administration of eight sessions of ECT without anesthesia. He was returned to Combinado del Este, from which he was released in 1979. In 1980 (about six months after his release), Guillén was accused of attempting to send abroad a document condemning human rights abuses by the Castro regime. Charged with "being dangerous to the Cuban Revolution," he was sentenced to four years in Combinado del Este Prison.

In November 1981, the political prisoner Rafael Saumell was transferred to the psychiatric ward of the Combinado del Este Prison hospital. There he met Guillén. Saumell later recalled that Guillén's doctor was Jesús Edreira, M.D.,[1] and that the nurse Natalia Figueroa forced Guillén to swallow several medications four times each day: twenty-five milligrams of

---

[1]This doctor is identified by Armando Valladares in his memoir *Against All Hope* as a psychiatrist in the Combinado del Este Prison hospital (New York: Alfred A. Knopf, 1986), p. 331.

chlorpromazine; trifluoperazine;[2] and trihexyphenidyl hydrochloride.[3] Each day, Figueroa would search Guillén's bunk to make sure he had not hidden the pills. Saumell remained in the ward with Guillén until May 1982, when he was transferred to La Cabaña Prison. Guillén was released in 1984.

From the time of his release from jail in 1984 until the end of 1989, Guillén's family kept him confined (on the recommendations of State Security) in the Havana Psychiatric Hospital (Mazorra) for six out of every seven days. He nonetheless remained active in the Cuban Committee for Human Rights (*Comité Cubano Pro Derechos Humanos*). At the end of 1989, he was allowed to emigrate to Miami, Florida. Since that time, he has become well-known in the emigré community for his paintings.

SOURCES

Affidavit, 4 October 1990.

Mary Jane Camejo, *Human Rights in Cuba: The Need to Sustain the Pressure* (Washington: Americas Watch, January 1989), pp. 86–87.

Interview, 13 April 1990.

Telephone Interview with Rafael Saumell, 18 November 1990.

---

[2] An anti-psychotic prescribed for "psychotic disorders [and] moderate to severe depression with anxiety. . . ." See Gilbert I. Simon, et. al., *The Pill Book*, Fourth Edition (New York: Bantam Books, 1990), pp. 886–889.

[3] An anti-Parkinsonian agent often used to prevent or control muscle spasms caused by phenothiazines. Its side effects include blurred vision, confusion, and an increased sensitivity to strong light. See *The Pill Book*, pp. 889–891.

THE HISTORIAN

Born on 20 March 1945 in Antilla, Oriente province, **Ariel Hidalgo Guillén** graduated with a degree in history from the University of Havana in 1975. He accepted an appointment to teach political science and economics to adults at the Manolito Aguiar Workers' High School in Havana. During the 1970s, he wrote several articles that were published in official Cuban journals. In 1976, he authored *Origins of the Workers' Movement and Socialist Thought in Cuba*, which was used as a university textbook in Cuba until 1981.

ARIEL HIDALGO GUILLÉN
OCCUPATION: HISTORY PROFESSOR
DIAGNOSIS: SANE
CONFINEMENT: 10 DAYS
ELECTROSHOCKS: NONE
PSYCHOTROPIC DRUGS: NO

His dissidence began on 3 July 1980, when he faced down a mob throwing rocks at one of his students, who was trying to leave Cuba during the Mariel boatlift. He was arrested, confined to State Security Headquarters at *Villa Marista* in Havana, and his home was searched. After three days of interrogation, he was released. When Hidalgo later applied for permission to leave Cuba, his application was refused and he was fired from his teaching position. Until his arrest in 1981, he was forced to earn a living by working in construction.

On 19 August 1981, Hidalgo was arrested and charged with "incitement against the social order, international solidarity and the Socialist State" under article 108-1 of the Cuban Penal Code. He was taken to *Villa Marista*, where he was held for the next twenty days. During a search of his home, State Security agents

71

found five copies of his manuscript, *Cuba, the Marxist State, and the New Class: A Dialectical Materialist Study*, which used an orthodox Marxist approach to criticize the Castro regime. At his half-hour-long trial, Hidalgo was called a "leftist revisionist;" his court-appointed attorney's defense consisted of saying that Hidalgo was "young and could change his views." Several members of his local Committee for the Defense of the Revolution (*Comité de Defensa de la Revolucíon,* or CDR) testified for the prosecution. (According to a 1986 Amnesty International report, their testimony consisted of saying that Hidalgo "talked too much.") He was found guilty and sentenced to eight years in prison. According to reports received by Americas Watch, the court also ordered that his books be burned.

On 9 September 1981, he was transferred from *Villa Marista* to the Carbó-Serviá ward of the Havana Psychiatric Hospital (Mazorra). He spent the next ten days with over one hundred dangerously psychotic inmates:

> I was placed in a [courtyard] closed off with iron bars . . . . Once inside, I realized I was at the complete mercy of a hundred men—convicts from different prisons, the overwhelming majority of whom were violently insane. . . . The doctors never crossed the shadows of the bars, and the orderlies only entered when they had to remove someone forcibly to be subjected to electroshock treatment. . . . I had to stand—not only because of the lack of space, but also because the floor was covered with excrement, saliva, sperm, et cetera. The most repulsive acts imaginable took place there, including rapes and beatings of defenseless elderly persons.

Hidalgo kept to himself as much as possible and tried to avoid provoking the other inmates.

At meal times, dozens of inmates would crowd the gate between the courtyard and the ward. When the gate opened, the inmates would charge for the dining hall:

72

> When you entered, the food already was on the tables.
> Plates were so close together to one another, that people
> had to climb on top of each other in order to eat. . . .
> Some inmates got two or three plates; the strong took the
> food away from the weak. Some, in their desperation to
> get one or two rations to eat, ran on top of the tables, step-
> ping on plates or knocking them to the ground.

Hidalgo ate only sporadically. Due to the quality of food and
the savagery of his fellow inmates, he found it difficult not to
vomit the food he did manage to eat. But for Hidalgo, the worst
was at night. He could not even close his eyes because he feared
that "some maniac would try and take advantage of my sleep
to commit some outrageous act." He lay awake, watching inmates pass the time by setting on fire the socks of their sleeping
companions. Some of the more deranged prisoners would mas-
turbate and urinate on those who slept. In his ten days in Carbó-
Serviá, he was taken out of the ward on only one occasion.

On 19 November 1981, he was transferred to Combinado
del Este Prison in Havana. For fourteen months — including the
first twelve he was there — he was kept in solitary confinement
in one of the cells of the prison's infamous "Rectangle of Death"
ward. During the last two years of his confinement, he twice
staged hunger strikes. During one of these strikes, authorities
took away his clothes and cut off his water.

On 4 August 1988, about one year before he was scheduled
to be discharged, Hidalgo was released from prison. On 12 August 1988, he was flown to Miami, Florida, where he now lives.

SOURCES

Amnesty International, *Cuba: Political Imprisonment—An Update* (London: Amnesty International, 1988), p. 2.

Amnesty International, *Cuba: Recent Developments Affecting the Situation of Political Prisoners and the Use off the Death Penalty* (London: Amnesty International, 1988), p. 30.

Amnesty International, *Political Imprisonment in Cuba* (London: Amnesty International, 1986), p. 12.

Mary Jane Camejo, *Human Rights in Cuba: The Need to Maintain the Pressure* (New York: Americas Watch, 1989), pp. 10–11; 83; 103.

Ariel Hidalgo, Interview witth Lourdes Meluza, 1990. Part of "Psychiatric Abuse in Cuba," a news series by WLTV-TV, Miami.

Nat Hentoff, "The Sadist as Revolutionary," *The Village Voice*, 1 July 1986.

Roger Lowenstein, "Loyal Marxist Languishes in Cuban Jail for Writing on Privileged 'Ruling Class,'" *The Wall Street Journal* (International Edition), 5 June 1985.

Antonio Ramirez, "Cuban Teacher Jailed by Revolution He Supported," *New York Teacher*, 1 September 1986.

Stephen J. Ritchin, et. al., *Human Rights in Cuba* (New York: Bar of the City of New York, 1988), pp. 35–37.

THE CIVIL SERVANT

Born in Bayamo on 21 August 1951, **Gualdo Hidalgo Portilla** graduated from Luis A. Turcios Lima High School in Bayamo. He first enrolled at Holguín University; he later transferred to the School of Humanities at the University of Santiago, from which he graduated in 1978 with a degree in philosophy.

GUALDO HIDALGO PORTILLA
OCCUPATION: CIVIL SERVANT
DIAGNOSIS: PARANOID SCHIZOPHRENIC
CONFINEMENT: 69 DAYS
ELECTROSHOCKS: 8–12
PSYCHOTROPIC DRUGS: YES

In 1976, Hidalgo was named a Professor of Philosophy at the Camilo Cienfuegos Vocational Military School in Holguín — despite the fact that he had not yet received his degree. By 1977, he had been promoted to Director of the Department of Philosophy. Later that same year, however, he was fired as a result of his failure to join the Communist youth. For the next year he taught training programs in the construction industry.

In October 1978, Hidalgo joined the Political Studies Department of the Provincial Power Assembly in Holguín, eventually being promoted to Department Chief. In this position, he was privy to policy briefings held in Havana on a wide variety of topics. It was his responsibility to explain new policies to provincial administrators, and to develop educational and training plans for the province. He also taught political economy and history of philosophy for state industry executives at the

75

National School of Economic Administration (*Escuela Nacional de Dirección de la Economía*) in Holguín.

Hidalgo still held these positions on 15 May 1981, when he sought asylum at the British Embassy in Havana. He was arrested by Cuban authorities, who accused him of attempting to kidnap the British Ambassador in order to obtain asylum. He was taken to State Security Headquarters at *Villa Marista* in Havana, where he was interrogated for twenty-seven days.

On 11 June 1981, Hidalgo was transferred to the Carbó-Serviá ward of the Havana Psychiatric Hospital (Mazorra). He was diagnosed as paranoid schizophrenic by Oscar de la Rosa, M.D. He remembers his experiences in Carbó-Serviá as the worst of his confinement: "Prison is nothing compared to Carbó-Serviá."

Hidalgo has stated that he received between eight and twelve electroshocks during his stay. He does not remember the exact figure because, as he later noted, "one of the characteristics of electroshock is that it erases short-term memory. When you receive several electroshocks, it is almost impossible to remember how many there were." The shocks were administered by a common prisoner with no professional training; often they were given to patients on a whim, sometimes as entertainment, sometimes as punishment.

Hidalgo was forced to ingest large doses of psychotropic drugs. He was unable to identify what the drugs were. Those who refused to take the drugs were threatened with beatings by gangs of criminally insane inmates. The combination of electroshocks and psychotropic drugs resulted in a number of side effects: memory loss; convulsions; muscular rigidity and a loss of muscular coordination; vertigo; and confusion. Hidalgo later commented that the large doses of psychotropic drugs "were more adequate to kill horses than to treat humans."

After sixty-nine days in Carbó-Serviá, Hidalgo was returned to *Villa Marista* on 20 August 1981, where he remained until 15 October 1981.

It continues to be unclear whether Hidalgo ever was tried or convicted of any crime. On 31 July 1981, the Cuban government announced that Hidalgo had been tried for his alleged actions at the British Embassy but had been found not guilty by reason of mental illness. Hidalgo since has stated, however that he never appeared before a tribunal or court of any kind. Despite his supposed exoneration, Hidalgo spent the next two years (October 1981 to sometime in 1983) at Combinado del Este Prison in Havana, and the following three years in the Provincial Prison in Holguín, from which he was released on the order of the Minister of Interior on 15 May 1986. Despite the claims of the Cuban government to the contrary, Hidalgo alleges that he was tried *in absentia* and convicted of "actions against the Chief of a Diplomatic Representation." To this day, he still does not know the terms of his conviction or sentence.

After his release from prison, Hidalgo survived by doing odd jobs in Holguín. He left for the United States on 13 June 1990. He lives in New Jersey with his wife and son, and has begun work as an operator in a print shop.

SOURCE

Written statement, 18 July 1990.

THE UNION ACTIVIST

JESÚS LEYVA GUERRA
OCCUPATION: SEAMAN
DIAGNOSIS: PARANOID SCHIZOPHRENIA
CONFINEMENT: 39 MONTHS
ELECTROSHOCKS: 24
PSYCHOTROPIC DRUGS: YES

Born in Santiago de Cuba in 1947, **Jesús Leyva Guerra** worked for many years as a seaman in the merchant marine. He became active in his union, and helped forward complaints about working conditions to the appropriate authorities. When they failed to respond, Leyva began to participate clandestinely in dissident activities. In 1978, Leyva was denounced by his brothers (who are State Security officials) for allegedly engaging in illegal foreign currency exchanges. He was sentenced to ten months in prison, the first seven of which he spent in the Havana Psychiatric Hospital (Mazorra). He completed his sentence at the Combinado del Este Prison in Havana.

In 1981, Leyva was arrested and charged with *salida ilegal,* attempting to leave Cuba illegally, under Article 247 of the Cuban Criminal Code. Sent to the Gustavo Machín Psychiatric Hospital (Jagua) in Santiago de Cuba, he was diagnosed as paranoid schizophrenic by Carmen Betancourt, M.D. and confined for two months. In 1983, Leyva was arrested for distributing dissident literature. Shipped once again to Machín, he was examined by Enrique Font, M.D., who rediagnosed him as paranoid schizophrenic. He was subjected to six sessions of electroconvulsive therapy in ten days. He was released after a three month confinement.

78

In 1985, Leyva was arrested and charged with attempting to seek asylum at the Ecuadorian Embassy in Havana. He was sentenced to three months in the Carbó-Serviá ward of the Havana Psychiatric Hospital. Transferred to Machín, he again was rediagnosed as paranoid schizophrenic by José Perez Milán, M.D., and given large doses of psychotropic drugs. He spent one month at Machín before being released. In 1986, while on a hunger strike to protest labor conditions at his place of work, Leyva was arrested and sent to Machín. Reexamined by Orlando Lamar-Vicens, M.D., the hospital's director of security, he was given six electroshocks and heavy doses of psychotropic drugs. He was released after five months.

In November 1987, Leyva was arrested moments after leaving the home of the human rights activist Elizardo Sánchez Santa Cruz. Confined for nine months in Machín, he was given a new psychiatric evaluation and additional doses of psychotropic drugs. On 14 July 1988, Leyva was arrested in Santiago de Cuba while collecting information for the Cuban Committee for Human Rights (*Comité Cubano Pro Derechos Humanos*) and the Cuban Commission for Human Rights and National Reconciliation (*Comisión Cubana de Derechos Humanos y Reconciliación Nacional*), two unofficial human rights groups operating within Cuba. Taken to Machín, he immediately began a hunger strike that would last eight days. Diagnosed once again by Lamar-Vicens, he was forced to undergo twelve sessions of electroconvulsive therapy and ingest large doses of psychotropic drugs. Leyva later stated that during this stay, he also suffered additional interrogations and beatings at the hands of Captain Carlos del Toro of the Ministry of Interior. He was confined to Machín for a total of nine months.

In *Human Rights in Cuba: The Need To Sustain the Pressure*, Americas Watch's Mary Jane Camejo states succinctly the hypocrisy not only of Leyva's confinement, but of confining any sane dissident to a psychiatric hospital:

> If Leyva has been confined to treat any mental illness he may suffer, why has he been held in the judicial ward of the hospital? If he has been held in the judicial ward because he has criminal charges pending against him, what are they? If it is because he is considered by judicial authorities to be dangerous to himself or to society, has he actually caused harm to himself or another person, or is this a form of preventive detention?

In an October 1989 interview with *Miami Herald* correspondent Liz Balmaseda, Leyva stated that the electroshocks and large doses of drugs were so frequent that he remembers very little of his stay. "Later they told me I ate on the eighth day of my hunger strike, but I don't remember." In a 1990 interview with Lourdes Meluza of WLTV-TV, Miami, he said that "the effects [of electroshock] included swelling of the lower and upper extremities and burned temples. . . . I was not able to recognize my family or my wife, and I secreted blood through my penis."

His wife, Elba, was horrified by what she found when she came to visit him at Mazorra. He was so disoriented that he failed to recognize her and sat down at a table with strangers. His arms and legs were swollen and his temples had electrode burns. "He was out of it, like a drunk, dead gone," she said later. "He would drool all over himself."

Elba and others complained to hospital officials, who told them that Leyva was "crazy" and that the hospital was trying to cure him. When *Los Angeles Times* correspondent Don Schanche asked a government official to comment on the complaints, the official "responded by shrugging his shoulders and rolling his eyes, then warned that it was dangerous for foreign journalists to interview human rights dissidents without first advising the government."

80

On 20 April 1989, after a little over nine months in detention, Leyva was released. In October 1989, he, along with his wife Elba and their two children, emigrated to the United States. They currently live in Miami, Florida.

SOURCES

Americas Watch, *Cuba: Jailing the Human Rights Movement* (New York: Americas Watch 1990), p. 1.

Liz Balmaseda, "The Mind of A Prisoner: The Case of an Exiled Activist Fuels Charges of Abuse in Cuban Psychiatric Hospitals," *The Miami Herald*, 25 October 1989.

Mary Jane Camejo, *Human Rights in Cuba: The Need to Sustain the Pressure* (New York: Americas Watch, 1989), pp. 30–31; 87–88; 104.

Jesus Leyva Guerra, Interview with Lourdes Meluza, 1990. Part of "Psychiatric Abuse in Cuba," a news series by WLTV-TV, Miami.

Don A. Schanche, "Cuban Rights Crackdown, Psychiatric Abuses Told," *The Los Angeles Times*, 12 January 1989.

Joseph B. Treaster, "Cuban Rights, Even Today, Are Not So Libre," *The New York Times*, 19 January 1989.

U.S. Department of State, *Country Reports on Human Rights Practices for 1989* (Washington: GPO, February 1990), p. 531.

THE MEDICAL STUDENT

ORESTES MARTÍNEZ HAYDAR
OCCUPATION: MEDICAL STUDENT
DIAGNOSIS: PARANOID SCHIZOPHRENIA
CONFINEMENT: 4 MONTHS
ELECTROSHOCKS: 16
PSYCHOTROPIC DRUGS: YES

Born in Havana on 15 February 1950, **Orestes Martínez Haydar** began medical school in 1968 at the University of Havana's Instituto de Ciencias Básicas Pre-Clínicas Victoria de Girón. On 21 September 1973, a month before graduation, he was expelled for "activities contrary to the revolution." Married, with two children, and with no chance of a job in medicine, he worked as a carpenter. His marriage began to fail, and he started suffering from depression.

In early September 1974, Martínez's wife called the police during a marital dispute. When Martínez refused to leave his house voluntarily, the police stormed it and took him to the Psychiatric Unit of the Calixto García Hospital in Havana. During his stay, he was attacked by another inmate and suffered adverse side effects from chlorpromazine. Martínez somehow managed to escape the hospital, steal a car, and drive to Fidel Castro's house, where he demanded to speak to Castro. He was arrested and taken to State Security Headquarters at *Villa Marista* in Havana. For the next two days, he was interviewed by Jorge López Valdez, M.D., the psychiatric advisor to State Security. Martínez was accused of trying to kill Castro, and transferred to the Castellanos ward of the Havana Psychiatric Hospital (Mazorra). When he refused to ingest psychotropic drugs dispensed by the orderly Heriberto Mederos, he was stripped and placed in solitary confinement. With the help of four aides, Mederos gave Martínez two electroshocks on a wet floor and without anesthesia or medical supervision.

After two days in Castellanos, Martínez was transferred to the Carbó-Serviá ward. There a young female psychiatrist di-

82

agnosed him as "violent" and ordered further electroconvulsive therapy (ECT). During his time in Carbó-Serviá, he was forced to undergo eleven sessions of ECT. According to Martínez, his experience was not the exception but the rule. Three times a week, at five o'clock in the morning, Mederos came to the ward and chose twenty to twenty-five inmates for electroconvulsive therapy. One by one, they were forced to accept a rubber bit in their mouth and held down on a wet floor often covered with the urine, vomit and excrement of those who had preceded them. Electrodes were attached to their bodies or heads, and electrical current was applied until they went into convulsions. Martínez since has stated that contrary to standard procedure, there were no follow-up evaluations to assess the therapy's effectiveness. Neither Martínez nor his family were notified of the reasons for the electroshocks, and he was not given the opportunity to refuse treatment.

After three months, Martínez was released in November 1974. He returned to work as a carpenter, but met with López Valdez regularly. In April 1976, in the midst of a bout with depression, he refused to work. His ex-wife, now a psychiatrist, had married a Ministry of Interior official during Martínez's internment. She diagnosed him as paranoid schizophrenic and had him recommitted to the Havana Psychiatric Hospital. In a ward adjacent to Carbó-Serviá, he received three electroshocks. He was given neither anesthesia nor muscle relaxants. On 17 May 1976, after a one month hospital stay, he was released. He left Cuba on 12 July 1978. In 1989, Martínez graduated with a Masters Degree in psychology from APEC University (*Asociación Pro-Educación y Cultura*) in the Dominican Republic, where he works as an industrial psychologist and personnel consultant.

SOURCE

Telephone interview, 4 May 1990.

THE TRUCK DRIVER

On the left, José Morales Rodríguez before he was sent to prison. On the right, Morales after his release.

JOSÉ MORALES RODRÍGUEZ
OCCUPATION: TRUCK DRIVER
DIAGNOSIS: NONE
CONFINEMENT: 18 DAYS
ELECTROSHOCKS: 14
PSYCHOTROPIC DRUGS: YES

Born in Victoria de las Tunas in 1939, **José Morales Rodríguez** was an independent truck owner-operator. In 1960, he was accused of conspiring against the government and sentenced to six years, which he served in the Boniato, Holguín and La Cabaña Prisons. Near the end of his term, a year was added because he would not cooperate with authorities. In 1970, he was arrested in Victoria de las Tunas and accused of conspiracy, serving one year in Holguín without a trial. In 1973, he again was arrested, serving nine months in Holguín and Santiago de Cuba Prisons without a trial. On 21 June 1981, he was arrested and accused of participating in a conspiracy to assassinate Fidel Castro. During his interrogation in Victoria de las Tunas, he was placed in a water tank and given electroshocks. In July, he was taken to the Gustavo Machín Psychiatric Hospital (Jagua) in Santiago de Cuba, where he was given fourteen electroshocks and large doses of psychotropic drugs. As a result, he experienced severe memory loss. After eighteen days in Machín, Morales was returned to Victoria de las Tunas and placed under house arrest, where he spent the next seven years.

In March 1989, he was allowed to leave Cuba. Today he lives in New Jersey, where he works in construction.

SOURCE

Interview, 11 April 1990.

84

THE EYE PATIENT

From left to right: Roberto Valero, the late Reinaldo Arenas, and Juan Peñate Fernández in Madrid, Spain (1986).

Born in 1939, **Juan Peñate Fernández** holds degrees in history and the classics from the University of Havana. In the 1970s, Peñate began to suffer from an eye problem requiring

JUAN PEÑATE FERNÁNDEZ
OCCUPATION: HISTORIAN
DIAGNOSIS: NONE
CONFINEMENT: 48 DAYS
ELECTROSHOCKS: NONE
PSYCHOTROPIC DRUGS: NO

a delicate operation only available to Cuban citizens in the Soviet Union and East Germany, and only after medical authorization. In the fall of 1978, the optometrist Orfilio Peláez, M.D. refused to support Peñate's application to travel to the USSR for the operation. Upon returning home, Peñate discussed his problem with a cousin. He became very upset, shouting that the Cuban authorities were crazy if they thought he would seek asylum in the USSR, as it was a worse place to live than Cuba. One of Peñate's neighbors, the president of the local Committee for the Defense of the

Revolution, overheard Peñate's remarks and denounced him to the authorities. (Peñate already had been detained briefly several times at State Security Headquarters at *Villa Marista* in Havana for his political activities.) The following day, Peñate was arrested and taken to the Vedado police station in Havana. Later that night, the authorities transferred him to the Carbó-Serviá ward of the Havana Psychiatric Hospital (Mazorra). Peñate later referred to the Carbó-Serviá and Castellanos wards as

> black holes. . . where prisoners are transferred. . . in order to make them manageable...through irresponsible applications of electroshock without medical supervision. . . wards in which the fantastic and the uniquely evil are joined: common thieves, murderers, and political prisoners come together.

Peñate later said that the authorities tried a variety of measures in order to destablize him. While he was not subjected to electroconvulsive therapy or psychotropic drugs, he was forced to watch three times per week while the orderly Heriberto Mederos gave electroshocks to political dissidents strapped to a wet floor. After forty-eight days, Peñate was released, only to discover he had been fired from his job as a researcher at the National Library in Havana. For the next two years Peñate fended off State Security's attempts to recruit him to inform on other intellectuals. On 5 April 1980, he sought political asylum at the Peruvian Embassy, leaving Cuba during the Mariel boatlift. He currently lives in Spain. He suffers from impaired vision and has fought throat cancer.

SOURCES

Roberto Valero, "Psiquiatría y Política en Cuba," *El Miami Herald (The Miami Herald)*, 12 July 1981.

Juan Peñate Fernández, "El Testimonio de un Cubano," *El Miami Herald (The Miami Herald)*, 25 August 1981.

Telephone interview, 20 September 1990.

THE ENVIRONMENTAL ACTIVIST

Born in Havana on 16 April 1943, **Orlando Polo González** attended González Lines High School in Havana. From 1971 to 1983, he worked as a graphic designer for the Ministry of Culture, a position he lost as a result of his dissidence. He also served as Director of the National School of Design from 1972 to 1974. He is president of the environmental and pacifist organization, *Sendero Verde* (Green Path), and is married to Mercedes Páez, who also is active in the peace and environmental movements. Until 1989,

ORLANDO POLO GONZÁLEZ
OCCUPATION: GRAPHIC DESIGNER
DIAGNOSIS: CHRONIC PARANOIA
CONFINEMENT: 12 DAYS
ELECTROSHOCKS: NONE
PSYCHOTROPIC DRUGS: NO

he and Páez lived at the headquarters of the Life Naturalist Association (*Asociación Naturista Vida*, or ANV), a vegetarian organization founded in 1935 by Spanish anarchists. The ANV operated as an officially sanctioned group of over one hundred fifty members, with its headquarters on a farm outside Havana.

In 1985, Polo began to hike through Cuba in order to talk about his environmental and pacifist ideals. After he met Páez in 1987, she often accompanied him. On roughly two dozen occasions, local authorities arrested or detained them briefly. In April 1988, as a result of their continued opposition to nuclear power and the war in Angola, the Cuban Supreme Court ordered the dissolution of *Asociación Naturista Vida* and the closing of its headquarters. On 17 September 1988, Polo and Páez testified

87

on behalf of both the ANV and *Sendero Verde* to the United Nations Commission on Human Rights delegation visiting Cuba.

On 21 August 1989, the police closed the ANV's farm headquarters, in the process detaining Polo and Páez for several hours. The farmhouse that served as Polo and Páez's home was sealed. Upon their release, Polo and Páez began a hunger strike. On 23 August, they were arrested and taken to State Security Headquarters at *Villa Marista*. Páez was released after two days. Polo was held for two weeks. He was interrogated without a defense attorney present.

On 22 September 1989, Polo again was arrested and held in *Villa Marista*. On 28 September, he was transferred to a punishment cell in the Castellanos ward of the Havana Psychiatric Hospital (Mazorra). Polo later charged that security officials posing as doctors took him to Castellanos, where he was forced to spend the following twelve days surrounded by criminally insane patients. He was diagnosed as suffering from "chronic paranoia, type A." In a telephone interview from Cuba conducted after his release by Lourdes Meluza of WLTV-TV in Miami, Polo described conditions in Castellanos as "horrible," comparing living conditions to those found in "a medieval cell." On October 9, he was taken back to *Villa Marista*, from which he was released without charge on 13 October 1989.

Upon his release, he was warned that if he persevered in his "dissident acts" he would be rearrested and accused of enemy propaganda. He nevertheless has continued to be active in environmental and pacifist causes. In March 1991, he was permitted to leave Cuba to visit the United States. He expects that the Cuban government will allow him to return.

SOURCES

Affidavit, Mrs. Lily Machado (sister), 5 July 1990.

Americas Watch, *Cuba: Jailing the Human Rights Movement* (New York: Americas Watch, 1990), p. 7.

Amnesty International, *Political Imprisonment in Cuba: A Summary of Amnesty International's Recent Concerns* (London: Amnesty International, 1989), p. 7.

Liz Baimaseda, "The Mind of a Prisoner," *The Miami Herald,* 25 October 1989.

Mary Jane Camejo, *Human Rights in Cuba: The Need to Sustain the Pressure* (New York: Americas Watch, 1989).

Orlando Polo, interview with Lourdes Meluza, 1990. Part of "Psychiatric Abuse in Cuba," a news series by WLTV-TV, Miami.

Orlando Polo, interview with Armando Lago, 11 March 1991.

Julia Preston, "Castro's Clamping Down Again," *The Washington Post,* 22 October 1989.

Ana E. Santiago, "Ecología de Cuba Avanza al Desastre, Dice Experto [Expert Says Ecology of Cuba Headed for Disaster]," *El Nuevo Herald (The Miami Herald),* 14 November 1990.

United Nations, Economic and Social Council, Centre for Human Rights. *Consideration of the Report of the Mission which Took Place in Cuba in Accordance with Commission Decision 1988/106* (Geneva: United Nations, 1989), p. 32.

United States Department of State, *Country Reports on Human Rights Practices, 1989* (Washington: GPO, 1990), p. 532.

THE MECHANIC

ANGEL TOMÁS QUIÑONES GONZÁLEZ
OCCUPATION: MECHANIC
DIAGNOSIS: UNKNOWN
CONFINEMENT: 1 YEAR
ELECTROSHOCKS: UNKNOWN
PSYCHOTROPIC DRUGS: UNKNOWN

Angel Tomás Quiñones González was born in Havana on 21 December 1950. After high school, he worked as an auto mechanic in a shop on Zanja Street in Havana.

In early 1972, he and fifty-six others were accused of conspiring to kill Fidel Castro and the Czech Ambassador. After being interrogated at State Security Headquarters at *Villa Marista* in Havana, he was held in La Cabaña Prison. On 5 February 1972, he was tried and convicted of actions "against the integrity and stability of the nation" (Case 98-72). He was sentenced to one year in prison, which he served at El Príncipe Prison in a ward with common criminals. He was released in February 1973.

From 1973 to 1989, as a result of his continued defiance as well as his alleged spraying of anti-Castro graffiti on walls throughout Havana, he was arrested, held, and released on numerous occasions. In early 1989 he was arrested and confined to the Carbó-Serviá ward of the Havana Psychiatric Hospital (Mazorra). Nothing is known of his confinement there.

On 9 March 1990 his badly burned body was found on hospital grounds. Authorities ruled that his death was due to asphyxiation by hanging, his body then having been doused with gasoline and set on fire. The Castro regime has blamed criminal-

90

ly insane patients in Mazorra. Quiñones' mother, Mrs. Reina González, has challenged this assertion, pointing to the unlikely presence of gasoline in a ward for the criminally insane as evidence of participation by hospital authorities. She also has stated that her son had no history of mental illness. Quiñones' body was not turned over to the family for burial until two full days after his death. At the funeral, government agents prevented the family from having an open casket.

SOURCES

Affidavit, Mrs. Reina González (mother), 24 September 1990.

"Ex preso muere ahorcado en hospital," *El Nuevo Herald (The Miami Herald),* 15 March 1990.

Government of Cuba. Ministry of Justice. Certificación de Antecedentes Penales [Certification of Earlier Imprisonment], 18 August 1986.

Telephone interview with Mrs. Reina González (mother), 24 April 1990.

THE ENGINEER

In 1988, after his release from prison and emigration to Miami, Andres Solares (left) met in Washington with several Members of Congress, including Senators Alfonse D'Amato (R-NY) and Bob Graham (D-FL).

ANDRÉS JOSÉ SOLARES TESEIRO
OCCUPATION: ENGINEER
DIAGNOSIS: NONE
CONFINEMENT: 3 DAYS
ELECTROSHOCKS: NONE
PSYCHOTROPIC DRUGS: NO

Born in 1946, **Andrés José Solares Teseiro** graduated from the University of Havana in 1968 with a degree in civil engineering. From 1969 to 1972, he received two UNESCO scholarships to pursue graduate work in port engineering and administration at the University of Wales in the United Kingdom. Upon returning to Cuba, he taught civil engineering and national economic management at the University of Havana and the Ministry of Higher Education. As a result of his criticism of the economic and political situation in Cuba, his courses were cancelled by the government.

In 1972, after an argument with the Minister of the Merchant Marine and Ports, he was arrested and held for twenty-four hours at State Security Headquarters in *Villa Marista*. In 1975, he again was arrested, this time for trying to organize a free labor union among the longshoremen. He was held for a little over a day at *Villa Marista*. In 1980, Solares began to organize the Cuban Revolutionary Party, whose ideology was based on the teachings of Cuban patriot José Martí. He wrote to United States Senator Edward M. Kennedy (D-MA), French President François Mitterand, and others, asking for advice. He also wrote to a cousin in the United States, and allegedly criticized the Cuban social system. Some of the letters were intercepted. On 22 December 1981, Solares was arrested. He spent the next two months under interrogation at *Villa Marista*.

On 17 February 1982, after repeated threats by his interrogators that he would be placed in a ward for the criminally insane if he did not provide evidence against other members of his new party, he was transferred to the Carbó-Serviá ward of the Havana Psychiatric Hospital (Mazorra). He was forced to fend for himself among over one hundred criminally insane inmates. During his stay, he saw authorities subject other inmates to indiscriminate electroconvulsive therapy and brutal beatings. After three days, thanks in large part to the protests of his family, he was sent back to *Villa Marista*. From *Villa Marista*, he was transferred to La Cabaña Prison.

On 13 May 1982, Solares was tried and convicted. He was not allowed to speak with his defense attorney before the trial, and was able to communicate with the attorney only through letters smuggled from prison by members of his family. The only evidence presented at the trial were his letters, as the witnesses called by the prosecution did not know anything about

93

his political activities or his new political party. He was sentenced to eight years, six of which he served in the La Cabaña and Combinado del Este Prisons. From October 1984 to November 1985, he was confined to a punishment cell.

After a worldwide campaign to obtain his freedom, he was released on 13 May 1988 and allowed to leave Cuba. He now resides in Miami, Florida, where he works as a Project Manager for Calmaquip Engineering Corporation, and writes for the Hispanic monthly *Ahora* and other newspapers. He is Vice President of the Cuban Revolutionary Party (*Autentico*) and a member of the National Directorate of the *Junta Patriótica Cubana*.

SOURCES

Affidavit, 4 July 1990.

Amnesty International, *Cuba: Political Imprisonment—An Update* (London: Amnesty International, 1988), p. 2.

Amnesty International, *Cuba: Recent Developments Affecting the Situation of Political Prisoners and the use of the Death Penalty* (London: Amnesty International, 1988), p. 31.

Amnesty International, *Political Imprisonment in Cuba* (London: Amnesty International, 1986), pp. 13–14.

Mary Jane Camejo, *Human Rights in Cuba: The Need to Sustain the Pressure* (New York: Americas Watch, 1989), p. 65; 105.

Telephone Interview, 12 April 1990.

THE COMPUTER SCIENTIST

Born on 12 December 1943 in Bayamo, Oriente province, **Julio Soto Angurel** graduated from the University of Havana in 1976 with a degree in Computer Science. He also took a job with the National Film Institute (*Instituto Cubano de Arte e Industria Cinematográfica,* or ICAIC) after graduating from high school. In 1970, he became the Director of the Special Effects Department at ICAIC. Later that same year, he was demoted to the repair shop for his opposition to the dismissal of a cameraman accused of homosexuality and for remarks about the cost of living in Cuba.

JULIO SOTO ANGUREL
OCCUPATION: COMPUTER SCIENTIST
DIAGNOSIS: UNKNOWN
CONFINEMENT: 6 WEEKS
ELECTROSHOCKS: UNKNOWN
PSYCHOTROPIC DRUGS: UNKNOWN

From 1971 to 1976, Soto worked at the Institute of Computer and Information Sciences at the University of Havana. In 1976, he was transferred to the *Escuela Superior de Guerra* (War College), where he served as a computer specialist. From 1976 to 1978, he served with the Cuban Armed Forces in Angola. Upon his return to Cuba, he went back to his job at the War College, where he remained until late 1988.

In 1988, after making public statements in support of *glasnost* and *perestroika*, he founded the José Martí Association of Independent Defenders of Human Rights and National Reconciliation (*Conjunto de Defensores Independientes de los Derechos Humanos y la Reconciliación Nacional, José Martí*). On 17 September 1988, he testified to the United Nations Commission on Human Rights delegation then visiting Cuba. As a result of his activities, he lost his job and had to earn a living as a dishwasher in a hospital.

On 8 October 1989, Soto was arrested in Havana. After being detained briefly at a local police station, he was transferred to the Havana Psychiatric Hospital (Mazorra), where he spent approximately six weeks in the Carbó-Serviá ward. He next was transferred to Combinado del Este Prison in Havana. At the time that this report went to press, he was believed to be held in solitary confinement in the *Los Candados* ward. In January 1990, Cuban authorities finally charged him with "contempt" and possession of explosives. He faces up to four years in prison, and remains in Combinado del Este.

SOURCES

Americas Watch, *Cuba: Jailing the Human Rights Movement* (New York: Americas Watch, 1990), p. 5.

Liz Balmaseda, "The Mind of a Prisoner: The Case off an Exiled Activist Fuels Charges of Abuse in Cuban Psychiatric Hospitals," *The Miami Herald* 25 October 1989.

Mary Jane Camejo, *Human Rights in Cuba: The Need to Maintain the Pressure* (New York: Americas Watch, 1989), p. 33.

Julia Preston, "Castro's Clamping Down Again," *The Washington Post*, 22 October 1989.

Telephone interview with Elena Granados (sister), 23 April 1990.

United States Department of State, *Country Reports on Human Rights Practices for 1989* (Washington: Government Printing Office, February 1990), p. 531.

THE MUSICIAN

Born on 28 December 1932, **Julio Vento Roberes** began studying music at age seven, graduating in 1948 from the *Academia Municipal de Música* in Matanzas. Vento was a flautist, composer, and soloist with the Matanzas Symphony Orchestra and National Orchestra of Cuba. His hobby was cartooning. On 27 August 1964, while attempting to leave Cuba, he was arrested in Havana and jailed for two years, first at La Cabaña and then at San Severino Castle. On 4 February 1977, Vento was arrested in Matanzas after

JULIO VENTO ROBERES
OCCUPATION: MUSICIAN
DIAGNOSIS: ACUTE PARANOIA
CONFINEMENT: 5 YEARS
ELECTROSHOCKS: 16
PSYCHOTROPIC DRUGS: YES

leaflets advocating political and civil rights and featuring his cartoons were posted throughout Matanzas. He was found guilty of distributing enemy propaganda under Article 108 of the Cuban Criminal Code and sentenced to five years in prison. Vento instead was committed to the Carbó-Serviá ward of the Havana Psychiatric Hospital (Mazorra) for the entire five year term. He was diagnosed as suffering from acute paranoia as well as "delusions that he was a defender of human rights." He was subjected to sixteen sessions of electroconvulsive therapy (ECT) and large doses of psychotropic drugs at the hands of the orderly Heriberto Mederos. Vento has said that when he showed the electrode burns on his forehead to Oscar de la Rosa, M.D., the attending psychiatrist, de la Rosa objected that the ECT had not been medically prescribed.

During the Mariel boatlift in 1980 (while Vento was in Mazorra), his wife was expelled from Cuba. This left Vento's children, Jesús (7 years old at the time) and Walkiria (2 years old) without parental supervision. At first, they lived with relatives. Cuban authorities eventually ordered them placed in the home of Juan Enrique Quin-tana Alvarez, a Ministry of the Interior official based in Matanzas, who formally adopted them. At the end of his term, Vento was not released. He again began to draw political cartoons. On 10 October 1982, while still in confinement, he was accused of distributing leaflets with anti-Castro caricatures and of writing letters abroad complaining that he had not been released from the Havana Psychiatric Hospital at the end of his term. He was found guilty of distributing enemy propaganda under Article 108 of the Cuban Criminal Code and sentenced to eight years in Combinado del Este Prison in Havana. Until early 1986, he was held with a group of *nuevos plantados*, but then was moved to another part of the prison. During his time in prison, he became a member of the Cuban Committee for Human Rights. In 1987, Vento was included on a list of prisoners to be released to a delegation from the U.S. Catholic Conference. Told he would have to leave without his children, he chose to remain in jail. On 22 August 1988, Vento was forcibly taken from prison and flown directly to the United States. He now lives in Tampa, Florida.

SOURCES

Affidavit, 18 October 1990.

Amnesty International, *Cuba: Political Imprisonment—An Update* (London: Amnesty International, 1988), p. 5.

Amnesty Intenational, *Cuba: Recent Developments Affecting the Situation of Political Prisoners* (London: Amnesty Intenational, 1988), pp. 31–32.

Mary Jane Camejo, *Human Rights in Cuba: The Need to Sustain the Pressure* (New York: Americas Watch, 1989), p. 88; p. 102.

THE CADET

Born in Havana on 30
September 1945, **Eduardo
Yanes Santana** attended
high school at José Ramón
Rodríguez Technological In-
stitute and as a cadet at Ceiba del Agua Military Academy.

EDUARDO YANES SANTANA
OCCUPATION: MILITARY CADET
DIAGNOSIS: UNKNOWN
CONFINEMENT: 1 MONTH
ELECTROSHOCKS: NONE
PSYCHOTROPIC DRUGS: YES

Upon graduation he enrolled in the School of Humanities of
the University of Havana, but did not graduate. Yanes was arrested on 13 April 1964 due to his opposition to compulsory
military service. Sent to La Cabaña Prison, he served two and
one-half months for insubordination and twelve months for failing to register for military service. He next was arrested in 1966
and held in isolation for forty-seven days in State Security Headquarters at *Villa Marista* in Havana. Transferred to a forced
labor battalion under the control of the Military Units to Aid
Production (UMAP), he was sent to a UMAP camp at KILO
9 near Morón, Camagüey province. Captured while trying to
escape, the authorities beat him savagely. In early 1967, as a
result of his continued defiance of UMAP authority, Yanes was
sent to the Camagüey Psychiatric Hospital. He was held for
four days and kept under constant sedation; no physician ever
diagnosed or treated him. After a failed escape attempt, he was
transferred first to La Cabaña and then to Morro Castle where
he served fifteen months.

Early in 1969 he was taken to the Habana del Este Naval
Hospital in Santa María del Mar, Havana province. He was examined by a group of psychiatrists and released. In the latter
half of 1969, he was accused of "failing to integrate into Marxist
society" and held for one month in the Castellanos ward of the
Havana Psychiatric Hospital (Mazorra). The orderly Heriberto

99

Mederos threatened him with electroshock treatments. Although Mederos did not carry out this threat, he did force Yanes to watch while he and one of his aides, a criminally insane inmate nicknamed "Caballo," gave electroshocks to others. Inmates were doused with water and forced to lie down on a wet floor. The shocks would continue until the inmate went into convulsions and became unconscious. Although it was winter, Yanes and the other detainees had to bathe outside with ice-cold water at five o'clock in the morning. Yanes also was forced to ingest psychotropic drugs. During his stay at the hospital, Yanes was not examined by a physician. Upon his release from Castellanos, he was confined for six months to El Príncipe Prison. One month into his stay, he was sentenced *in absentia* to an additional eighteen months for being "highly dangerous." He spent the last four months of this sentence in the Quivicán Penal Prison.

Late in 1978, Yanes was held for ten days at State Security Headquarters in *Villa Marista*. While there, agents attempted to recruit him to spy on other dissidents. In 1980, Yanes was one of many who sought asylum at the Peruvian Embassy.[1] He left for Costa Rica on 16 April 1980 and came to the United States on 12 July 1980. Before his departure, all of his manuscripts were confiscated. He now resides in Miami, Florida, where he owns and manages a ceramic tile installation firm. He is completing work on a collection of his poems and a memoir of events at the Peruvian Embassy.

SOURCES

Affidavit, 6 July 1990.

Telephone interview, 27 April 1990.

---

[1] Thousands sought asylum in the Embassy. This event began a chain of events that resulted in the massive Mariel boatlift to the United States.

THE PHYSICIAN

Born on 4 May 1946 in Holguín, Oriente province, **Fulgencio Mario Zaldívar Batista** attended the Instituto de Holguín and the Marist Brothers High School in Holguín. He studied medicine at the University of Oriente, later transferring to the University of Havana, from which he graduated as a Doctor of Medicine in 1972. Zaldívar practiced sports medicine, later working in the Aleida Fernández Cherdie polyclinic in Marianao, a municipality in Havana Province.

F. MARIO ZALDÍVAR BATISTA
OCCUPATION: PHYSICIAN
DIAGNOSIS: ANXIETY
CONFINEMENT: 15 DAYS
ELECTROSHOCKS: NONE
PSYCHOTROPIC DRUGS: YES

On 20 December 1979, Zaldívar was arrested at the Barlovento Marina and accused of attempting to leave the country illegally under Article 247 of the Cuban Criminal Code. During his initial detention and interrogation at State Security Headquarters at *Villa Marista* in Havana, he was tortured and confined to an ice-cold cell.

On 14 March 1980, he was transferred to the Havana Psychiatric Hospital (Mazorra). He was diagnosed as suffering from anxiety and confined to the Carbó-Serviá and Castellanos wards. Each day, Zaldívar and the other inmates were forced to swallow a one hundred milligram tablet of chlorpromazine:

> Everyone was forced to take the pill. They would look into our mouths to make sure that we swallowed it. If we didn't, criminally insane inmates would beat us up in return for privileges granted by the staff.

101

Zaldívar experienced mental confusion, disorientation, drowsiness, weakness, incoherence, and diarrhea as a result of the chlorpromazine.

Since his release, Zaldívar has discussed some of the things he witnessed while at Mazorra: gross and indiscriminate use of psychotropic drugs, usually administered forcibly by other inmates; inhuman living conditions; the use of psychiatric techniques against sane individuals; and the mixing of political dissidents with the criminally insane. Zaldívar also has emphasized that he found it particularly disturbing that all of this was being done under the supervision of professional medical personnel. After fifteen days in Mazorra, Zaldívar was returned to *Villa Marista* for twelve days of interrogation. Blindfolded with a black hood over his head and bound by a rope tied tightly around his neck, he was beaten and kicked until he lost consciousness. He eventually was transferred to the Combinado del Este Prison in Havana where, eighteen months after his arrest, he was told that he had been sentenced *in absentia* to four years in prison. From May 1980 to early 1982, he was confined to Combinado del Este. During his stay there he experienced cardiac valve problems as a result of bacterial endocarditis. He then served six months in La Cabaña Prison. The final two years of his sentence were spent in Holguín and Playa Manteca Prisons. Zaldívar was released at the end of 1983. On 18 December 1985, he left Cuba for Panama. He now resides in Miami, Florida, where he is studying for the Medical Board exams. He has published a book of poems composed in prison.

SOURCES

Armando Valladares, *Contra Toda Esperanza [Against All Hope]* (Barcelona: Plaza & Janes, Editores S.A., 1985), p. 442.

Written Statement, 3 July 1990.

III

EMERGING CASES

Whenever possible, the authors have verified cases through independent sources. There were, however, six cases where this was not feasible. In four cases—those of Leandro Hidalgo Pupo, Marcos Miranda Morales, Francisco Tejera Garrido, and Manuel Tejera Garrido—the authors were not able to determine whether the victims were confined because of their political beliefs or because of genuine psychiatric problems. In the case of Emilio Montero Romero, the authors could not corroborate reports of psychiatric abuse through independent sources. Finally, the case of Samuel Martínez Lara is based in part on his belief that he might have been given psychotropic drugs during an interrogation.

The authors nonetheless feel that these cases merit inclusion in the report: until the Castro regime allows a thorough and independent investigation into these cases, the evidence available remains sufficiently compelling to regard these individuals as victims of abuse.

In addition, four new cases emerged as this report was about to go to press. Due to space considerations, only brief summaries of these cases could be included, and the relevant information could not be incorporated into the overview.

THE BOXING FAN

Leandro Hidalgo Pupo (center) is arrested by Cuban officials after shouting "Down with the dictatorship of Castro" during an internationally televised boxing match in Havana. [Photo: Agence France Presse]

On 23 February 1990, before thousands of spectators attending an internationally televised boxing match at the Sports City Coliseum in Havana, **Leandro Hidalgo**

LEANDRO HIDALGO PUPO
OCCUPATION: UNKNOWN
DIAGNOSIS: PARANOID SCHIZOPHRENIA
CONFINEMENT: BELIEVED STILL CONFINED
ELECTROSHOCKS: UNKNOWN
PSYCHOTROPIC DRUGS: UNKNOWN

Pupo, who is twenty years old, shouted "down with Fidel Castro" and "down with the dictatorship of Fidel Castro." He was beaten, dragged away from the ring, and arrested. According to rumors circulating in Havana, Hidalgo suffered cerebral swelling and drainage as a result.

Two months later, Amnesty International received reports that after a brief stay in *Villa Marista*, Hidalgo was transferred to the Carbó-Serviá ward of the Havana Psychiatric Hospital. There he was diagnosed as suffering from "paranoid schizo-

105

phrenia with moderate personality defects [*esquizofrenia paranoide con defectos moderatos de personalidad*]." He is under the supervision of José Perez Milán, M.D., and is being detained without trial. As of December 1990, it was unclear whether he continued to be held in Mazorra.

SOURCES

Pablo Alfonso, "Fuentes: Recluido por vocear contra Castro," *El Nuevo Herald (The Miami Herald)* 10 May 1990.

Amnesty International, *Cuba: The Human Rights Situation* (London: Amnesty International, 1990), pp. 22–23.

"Havana Psychopathy," Editorial, *The Miami Herald,* 15 May 1990.

THE PSYCHIATRIST

Born in 1952, **Samuel Martínez Lara** graduated in 1974 from the University of Oriente with a degree in medicine. In 1976, he did graduate work in community mental health at the University of California (Berkeley). Upon his return to Cuba, he worked as a psychiatrist at the Calixto García Hospital in Havana.

SAMUEL MARTÍNEZ LARA
OCCUPATION: PSYCHIATRIST
DIAGNOSIS: "PSYCHOPATHY"
CONFINEMENT: NOT APPLICABLE
ELECTROSHOCKS: NONE
PSYCHOTROPIC DRUGS: UNKNOWN

In 1982, the head of State Security in Calixto García demanded that Martínez Lara give him the file on one of Martínez Lara's patients. When Martínez Lara refused, he was arrested and accused of having been recruited to work for the CIA while at Berkeley. His (then) wife, Teresa Mayans, and her son by a previous marriage, Salvador Blanco, also were arrested and charged with "planning to leave Cuba illegally" under Article 247 of the Cuban Penal Code.

On 15 October 1982, he was tried, convicted, and sentenced to three years in Combinado del Este Prison in Havana. While in prison, he met Ricardo Bofill, Elizardo Sánchez, and other human rights activists, and joined the Cuban Committee for Human Rights (*Comiteé Cubano Pro Derechos Humanos*, or CCPDH). He was released on 11 April 1985.

After his release, Martínez Lara continued to work on behalf of the CCPDH. In mid-September 1986, he was arrested and accused of public disorder. Held for 137 days at State Security Headquarters in *Villa Marista* in Havana, he was not brought to trial.

During his stay in *Villa Marista*, Martínez Lara's interrogators told him he had to be insane to oppose the government, warned him that they would transfer him to the forensic wards of the Havana Psychiatric Hospital (Mazorra), and threatened to subject him to electroconvulsive therapy without anesthesia. Martínez Lara also believes that psychotropic drugs might have been mixed in with his food. During his stay at *Villa Marista*, he developed an involuntary tremor in his lips, tongue, and face. Such symptoms are not unlike those found in patients with tardic dyskinesia, potentially irreversible, involuntary purposeless tremors that are a common side effect of psychotropic drugs. However, Martínez Lara did not uncover any physical evidence (such as half-dissolved tablets in his food) that would confirm his suspicions.

After he was released in February 1987, Martínez Lara continued to be active in the CCPDH. In mid-1988, he co-founded the Human Rights Party of Cuba (*Partido Pro Derechos Humanos de Cuba* or PPDHC) and became publisher of *Franqueza* (*Frankness*), its two-page *samizdat* newsletter. In September 1988, Martínez Lara testified on limitations placed by the Cuban government on the right of asylum before the delegation from the United Nations Commission on Human Rights then visiting Cuba. He also submitted written testimony documenting individuals who had suffered reprisals as a result of their attempts to emigrate. In November 1988, after Tania Díaz Castro, the PPDHC's Secretary-General, was arrested, Martínez Lara became acting Secretary-General.

On 29 March 1989, Martínez Lara, his fiancée Maria Elena Otero, and six others were arrested and charged with "clandestine printing" (*clandestindad de impresos*) under article 210 of the Cuban Penal Code. On 30 March, the eight were tried at the *Tribunal Municipal Popular de Centro Habana*. Martínez Lara was convicted, fined three hundred pesos, and released. On 2 April, Martínez Lara was interviewed by CBS; the interview subsequently appeared on the *CBS Evening News*. Martínez Lara told the network that the Cuban government was "the most cruel and repressive regime on the continent." On 1 April, Martínez Lara and other PPDHC leaders publicly announced that they intended to hold a demonstration outside the Soviet Embassy on occasion of Soviet President Mikhail Gorbachev's visit to Havana.

The following day, Martínez Lara, Roberto Bahamonde Masot, and at least nine others were arrested in a pre-dawn raid on their homes. Martínez Lara was charged with being a "person dangerous to socialist society." His trial was closed to the public, and he was not allowed the benefit of legal counsel. On 7 April 1989, he was sentenced to nine months in prison, which he served in Aguica Prison in Matanzas. Although his term was set to expire on 4 January 1990, prison authorities informed him that he would not be released, and that they were charging him with "contempt for Fidel Castro," and with making offensive comments regarding Panama. On 27 February 1990, his sentence was commuted to "conditional liberty" as provided for by Article 34 of the Cuban Criminal Code.[1]

On 5 March 1990, Martínez Lara was one of several members of the CCPDH and the PPDHC who were meeting at the home of Sebastián Arcos Bergnes when a mob attacked the house in an "act of repudiation." According to a recent Am-

---

[1]Those sentenced to conditional liberty can live at home and go to work, but cannot change their residence without permission. Their behavior and actions are monitored closely by their local Committee for the Defense of the Revolution. For more on conditional liberty, see Human Rights Watch, *The Persecution of Human Rights Monitors: A Worldwide Survey* (New York: Human Rights Watch, December 1990), p. 34n.

nesty International report, the meeting was interrupted when "large crowds of civilians attacked the house over a period of several hours while members of the Cuban security forces stood by." Americas Watch reported that the mob "broke down the door of [Arcos's] home without entering, broke windows, hurled insults, and shouted revolutionary slogans." Five days later (10 March), Martínez Lara, Díaz Castro, and seven other PPDHC members were arrested. In July, Díaz Castro and one other PPDHC member, after weeks of interrogation, broke down and agreed to cooperate. They appeared on television and stated that the Cuban human rights movement was being manipulated by foreign governments in order to undermine Cuban socialism. Two months later, they and six of the seven PPDHC members arrested in March were released pending trial.

The exception was Martínez Lara, who remained incarcerated in isolation in State Security Headquarters at *Villa Marista* in Havana for the next eleven months. His interrogators subjected him to repeated and brutal beatings. In May 1990, Martínez Lara was transferred to the Havana Psychiatric Hospital (Mazorra), where two psychiatrists interviewed him in a room adjacent to the Carbó-Serviá ward. He also was given an electroencephalogram (EEG). After less than twenty-four hours in Mazorra, he was transferred back to *Villa Marista*. During his various incarcerations, he has developed respiratory and circulatory ailments that became so severe that toward the end of his imprisonment, he was unable to walk. In August, he was transferred to a hospital, where he remained for one week.

On 5 February 1991, Martínez Lara was tried on charges of rebellion and crimes against state security. At his trial, the two psychiatrists who had interviewed him for a few hours the previous May testified that he was a "psychopath with personality disorders." He was convicted and sentenced to three years of conditional liberty. In June 1991, Martínez Lara and Maria

Elena Otero were expelled from Cuba. They now are living in Miami, Florida.

SOURCES

Affidavit, Teresa Mayans (ex-wife), 28 January, 1991.

Americas Watch, *Cuba: Jailing the Human Rights Movement* (New York: Americas Watch, 1990), p. 10.

Americas Watch, *Human Rights Activists behind Bars* (New York: Americas Watch, 1989), pp. 2–4.

Amnesty International, *Cuba: Recent Developments Affecting the Situation of Political Prisoners and the use of the Death Penalty* (London: Amnesty International, 1988), p. 20.

Amnesty International, *Medical Concern: Dr. Samuel Martínez Lara (Cuba)* (London: Amnesty International, 14 November 1990), pp. 1–2.

Alfonso Chardy, "Dissidents Arrested in Havana," *The Miami Herald*, 5 April 1989.

Interview, Samuel Martínez Lara, 9 July 1991.

U.N. Economic and Social Council, Commission on Human Rights, *Consideration of the Report of the Mission which Took Place in Cuba in Accordance with Commission Decision 1988/106.* (Geneva: United Nations, 1989), pp. 32–34.

THE SCRIPTWRITER

MARCOS MIRANDA MORALES
OCCUPATION: SCRIPTWRITER
DIAGNOSIS: STRESS
CONFINEMENT: 2 MONTHS
ELECTROSHOCKS: 7
PPYCHOTROPIC DRUGS: NO

A scriptwriter, director, and actor for the Cuban Institute of Radio and Television (*Instituto Cubano de Radio y Televisión* or ICRT), **Marcos Miranda Morales** was born in Havana on 24 September 1938. He is a graduate of Colegio El Salvador High School and holds a degree in Scenic Arts from the *Instituto Superior del Arte* (Art Institute) in Havana.

On 2 September 1980, in the aftermath of the Mariel boatlift, Miranda was summoned to State Security headquarters at *Villa Marista* in Havana. Moisés Vega of the Operations Department of the Interior Ministry tried to recruit Miranda to be a State Security agent inside Cuban television. When Miranda refused, the ICRT fired him. He was forced to perform menial labor to make a living. State Security continued to pressure him, and tried to blackmail him by warning that his wife and brother, both of whom also worked for the ICRT, would lose their jobs if he did not cooperate.

In March 1983, he was confined to the Enrique Cabrera General Teaching Hospital in Havana for symptoms related to stress. One of the staff psychiatrists, Francisco Murias M.D., accused Miranda of faking his illness to avoid work and prescribed treatment involving seven sessions of electroconvulsive therapy. His stay in Cabrera lasted for two months.

112

Miranda left Cuba for the United States in October 1984. He currently works for the United States Information Agency's Radio Martí Program in Miami, Florida as a writer of comedy scripts. For several years he has been attempting to secure an exit visa from the Cuban government for his twenty-six year old daughter, Cristina Miranda Cotolí, who has a Spanish entry visa.

SOURCES

Affidavit, 21 November 1990.

Telephone interview, 18 April 1990.

THE FARMER

EMILIO MONTERO ROMERO
OCCUPATION: FARMER
DIAGNOSIS: NONE
CONFINEMENT: 7 DAYS
ELECTROSHOCKS: UNKNOWN
PSYCHOTROPIC DRUGS: UNKNOWN

A farmer (*campesino*), **Emilio Montero Romero** was born in 1934, and is married with two children. On 14 November 1986, he was accused of organizing a conspiracy to kill Fidel Castro in the towns of Melena del Sur and Alquízar, Havana province, taken to State Security Headquarters in *Villa Marista*, and placed in solitary confinement for the next two days. He then was placed in the Havana Psychiatric Hospital (Mazorra) for seven days before being returned to *Villa Marista*.

During his first stay in *Villa Marista*, Montero was subjected to as many as ten or twelve separate interrogations each day. His interlocutors insulted him repeatedly. When Montero tried to respond, they beat him. On one occasion, Montero told an interrogator that he "couldn't take it anymore." The interrogator responded by handing Montero a loaded gun with which to shoot himself. Montero later said he returned the gun "because I didn't know how to use it and because I didn't have the courage to kill myself."

The day after this incident, Montero's interrogators forcibly injected him with an unknown substance. The following day, he was transferred to the Carbó-Serviá ward of the Havana Psychiatric Hospital (Mazorra), where a panel of psychiatrists prescribed that he be given electroconvulsive therapy. He protested vividly that he was sane, and caused such a commotion that authorities transferred him to the punishment cells of the Castellanos ward. He spent seven days in a small, unlit, and unfurnished cell. Every night, an insane inmate—who Montero believes worked for State Security—drenched him with water through a small opening in the door. Montero later said that he did not sleep during his stay.

114

After a week at Castellanos, Montero was returned to *Villa Marista*. During interrogation, State Security agents warned him that if he did not sign a self-incriminating confession, he never would see his family again. Montero broke down and signed the confession.

Montero later described how his experiences in Mazorra and *Villa Marista* had affected him:

> I am destroyed. Anything can make me cry. I cannot sleep well. I am extremely nervous, and I fear what they might still do to me. . . . Listen, we have been kidnapped. . . . I don't like the government, but I have never participated in politics. I haven't done anything against communism or against Batista or against anybody. All I do is live for my work. . . . When I was a farmer (*campesino*), I frequently heard about such things [as torture]. But everything I heard is far less than what I imagined. I still think that what has happened to me isn't true. I'm living a nightmare from which I haven't awakened. This is hell.

On 25 September 1987, he was transferred to the Combinado del Este Prison in Havana, where he reportedly remains today.

SOURCE

Emilio Montero Romero, Interview with Sandor Mendoza in "A la Sombra de un Evento [Under the Shadow of an Event]," *Aurora*, No. 7 (September–October 1987), pp. 10–14. *Aurora* is a *samizdat* publication, published clandestinely by political prisoners in the Combinado del Este Prison in Havana.

THE BROTHERS

MANUEL TEJERA GARRIDO
OCCUPATION: UNKNOWN
DIAGNOSIS: APATHETIC TO SOCIALISM
CONFINEMENT: 1 WEEK
ELECTROSHOCKS: UNKNOWN
PSYCHOTROPIC DRUGS: UNKNOWN

FRANCISCO TEJERA GARRIDO
OCCUPATION: UNKNOWN
DIAGNOSIS: UNKNOWN
CONFINEMENT: AT LEAST ONE YEAR
ELECTROSHOCKS: UNKNOWN
PSYCHOTROPIC DRUGS: UNKNOWN

Born in 1967, **Manuel Tejera Garrido** decided in 1988 to escape Cuba in a raft he and six friends built out of rubber tires. He told his mother that he "would rather be eaten by sharks and die than continue to live under Castro." In mid-August 1988, the seven set out for Florida. On 21 August, they were captured twenty-two miles off the Cuban coast and charged under Article 247 of the Cuban Criminal Code with "illegal exit." After being interrogated in State Security Headquarters at *Villa Marista* in Havana, Manuel was characterized as "apathetic to socialist society" and transferred to the Carbó-Serviá ward of the Havana Psychiatric Hospital (Mazorra). He spent the following seven days there among criminally insane inmates, and, according to his mother, was officially diagnosed as "apathetic to socialism." He currently is interned at Combinado del Este Prison in Havana.

Manuel's brother, **Francisco Tejera Garrido**, was confined to the Psychiatric Unit of the Havana del Este Naval Hospital (Third Floor, Ward G, Bed 17) on 5 September 1988 after he refused to serve in the military. Cuban authorities have stated that he will remain in the hospital's psychiatric unit for a period equal to his military service obligation.

SOURCE

Written statement of Mrs. Juana Garrido Ojeda (mother) submitted to the United Nations Commission on Human Rights, 1 November 1988, as reprinted in Ricardo Bofill, editor, *Cuba 1988: Situación de los Derechos Humanos* (Miami: Comité Cubano Pro Derechos Humanos, 1989), p. 126.

116

Reportedly a member of the Cuban national handball team, **Juan Barzaga Santacruz** was arrested while participating in a demonstration in Havana Central Park.

JUAN BARZAGA SANTACRUZ
OCCUPATION: ATHLETE
DIAGNOSIS: UNKNOWN
CONFINEMENT: 9 MONTHS
ELECTROSHOCKS: UNKNOWN
PSYCHOTROPIC DRUGS: UNKNOWN

According to reports received by Amnesty International, Barzaga and about forty others gathered to hear the reading of a statement that called for a democratic opening in Cuba. Barzaga reportedly sat down on the monument to Cuban national hero José Martí and stated that he would not move until a plebiscite was held in Cuba. Amnesty reports that Barzaga spent the following nine months in the Carbó-Serviá ward of the Havana Psychiatric Hospital (Mazorra). It is not clear whether he remains there today.

SOURCE

Amnesty International, *Cuba: The Human Rights Situation* (London: Amnesty International, 1990), p. 22.

• • • • •

A member of the Cuban Committee for Human Rights (*Comité Cubano Pro Derechos Humanos*, or CCPDH), and their first delegate in the muni-

OSCAR PEÑA RODRÍGUEZ
OCCUPATION: UNKNOWN
DIAGNOSIS: "DANGEROUSNESS"
CONFINEMENT: UNKNOWN
ELECTROSHOCKS: UNKNOWN
PSYCHOTROPIC DRUGS: UNKNOWN

cipality of Mella, Santiago de Cuba, **Oscar Peña Rodríguez** reportedly was confined on 12 December 1989. Amnesty International has reported that he was taken to the "Jagua ward" of the local psychiatric hospital. This in all likelihood is the Gustavo Machín Psychiatric Hospital in Santiago de Cuba, which also is known by its pre-revolutionary name of Jagua. His wife reportedly was shown a document certifying that he had been confined because he posed a danger to society (*"peligrosidad,"* literally "dangerousness"). There are unconfirmed reports that while in Jagua, he was confined for sixty-five days in a punish-

ment cell after he tried to help other patients. There also are unconfirmed reports that Cuban authorities threatened him with electroconvulsive therapy. While he has been released, it is not clear when he was released, or for how long he was detained.

SOURCE

Amnesty International, *Cuba: The Human Rights Situation* (London: Amnesty International, 1990), p. 22.

. . . . .

LUIS ALBERTO PITA SANTOS
OCCUPATION: PROFESSOR
DIAGNOSIS: "MENTAL ALIENATION"
CONFINEMENT: AT LEAST 26 DAYS
ELECTROSHOCKS: UNKNOWN
PSYCHOTROPIC DRUGS: UNKNOWN

A former professor of Marxism-Leninism at the *Instituto Superior Pedagógico de la Educación Técnica y Profesional* in Havana, **Luis Alberto Pita Santos**, 43, is a member of the Cuban Commission for Human Rights and National Reconciliation (*Comisión Cubana de Derechos Humanos y Reconciliación Nacional,* or CCDHRN). In March and April 1990, he was detained briefly on two occasions. On 1 May 1990, authorities searched his home. After allegedly finding a number of "incriminating" documents, they arrested him and charged him with "clandestine printing." He was provisionally released pending a psychiatric evaluation. Amnesty International has received reports that on eight separate occasions over the past four years, Pita Santos has been detained and referred to psychiatric authorities for evaluation. In July, the Mariano's Peoples Court acquitted him on the grounds that he was "in a state of mental alienation [*en estado de enajenación mental*]." On 27

118

August 1990, Pita Santos issued an open letter in which he charged that twenty-seven individuals, including his former employers, party officials, judges and the staff of the Havana Psychiatric Hospital, had committed a variety of offenses, including falsification of documents. He also stated in the same letter that while the staff of the Carbó-Serviá ward of the Havana Psychiatric Hospital had treated him well, the version of their report given to the Mariano Peoples Court was not the same one given to him. On 28 August 1990, the day after he issued the open l⌐ ter, Pita Santos was re-arrested and confined in State Security headquart⌐ s at *Villa Marista* in Havana. On 3 September 1990, he was recommitted to the Carbó-Serviá ward of the Havana Psychiatric Hospital, where he reportedly spent the next twenty-six days. As Amnesty has noted, it remains unclear whether Pita Santos was confined because of his human rights activities or because he genuinely needed psychiatric care. It also is unclear whether any abuse occurred during his confinement(s).

> ## SOURCE
>
> Amnesty International, *Cuba: The Human Rights Situation* (London: Amnesty International, 1990), p. 22.

. . . . .

The writer **Rafael Saumell Muñoz** was arrested in 1981 and charged with enemy propaganda. In December 1981, while awaiting trial in La Cabaña Prison, Saumell

RAFAEL SAUMELL MUÑOZ
OCCUPATION: WRITER
DIAGNOSIS: NEUROTIC ANXIETY
CONFINEMENT: 20 MONTHS
ELECTROSHOCKS: NONE
PSYCHOTROPIC DRUGS: YES

attempted suicide. After a brief stay in the prison infirmary, he was taken to the psychiatric ward of the Combinado del Este Prison Hospital and placed in the care of Jesús Edreira González, M.D., the psychiatrist in charge of the ward. Four times each day, Saumell was given drugs such as trifluoperazine and chlor-

119

promazine. He remained confined to the ward until December 1982, when he was returned to La Cabaña. In July 1985, Saumell and a number of other political prisoners were transferred from Guanajay Prison to Combinado del Este Prison, where they were interned with common criminals. In protest, the political prisoners began a hunger strike, electing Saumell to negotiate with prison authorities. Identified by prison authorities as a troublemaker, Saumell was interrogated by a State Security Captain named Alexis (Saumell does not remember his first name). Alexis told Saumell that since leading a hunger strike could add up to eight years to his sentence, Saumell must be suffering a relapse of his earlier psychiatric problems to be so foolish as to lead such a strike one year before his sentence was scheduled to expire. A few days later, Alexis' threat became reality when Saumell was transferred to the Psychiatric Ward of the Combinado del Este Prison Hospital and placed under the care of Digna Martínez, M.D., the new director of the ward who had signed his internment order. Allegedly an official in the Ministry of Interior, Martínez diagnosed Saumell as suffering from neurotic anxiety and prescribed additional psychotropic drugs. When Saumell questioned her diagnosis, Martínez laughed and told Saumell that it meant "he was contradictory and trusted no one," and that only State Security could authorize his release from the ward. In April 1986, Saumell was discharged from the psychiatric ward and released from prison. He now resides in St. Louis, Missouri, where he is completing a doctorate in Spanish literature.

IV

APPENDIX

CUBAN RIGHTS CRACKDOWN, PSYCHIATRIC ABUSES TOLD

DON A. SCHANCHE

HAVANA—The Cuban government has launched a new crackdown against human rights activists and for the first time stands accused of using electric shock treatments and psychoactive drugs against forcibly hospitalized political prisoners, according to leaders of the country's two major human rights groups.

After more than a year of grudging official tolerance of the groups, beatings, arrests, and surveillance of human rights workers have accelerated since mid-September, said Elizardo Sánchez, head of the Cuban Commission for Human Rights and National Reconciliation, and Sebastián Arcos Bergnes, vice president of the Cuban Human Rights Committee. At the same time, Sánchez and Arcos charged in separate interviews, widespread rights abuses, including at least one unprovoked police killing of a minor offender, have again increased under the regime of Fidel Castro.

The leaders of the groups, which are technically illegal, called the crackdown "renewed repression" and said that, ironically, the beginning of the trend coincided with a ten-day investigation last September by a delegation from the U.N. Human Rights Commission.

Reprinted with Permission from The Los Angeles Times, *12 January 1989.* *Copyright 1989 The Times Mirror Corporation.*

The U.N. Commission's visit had aroused hope among many observers for a further easing of government pressure against dissidents. A formal report of the inquiry has not yet been written, but members of the U.N. group had been quoted as reporting that they found fewer rights abuses in Cuba than they had expected. The charges of psychiatric abuse against political prisoners, once common in the Soviet Union but never before reported in Cuba, came from both human rights groups, acting independently. Each said it had forwarded its information to the U.N. Commission and to independent rights groups such as Americas Watch and Amnesty International.

Arcos said the best documented case is that of Jesús Leyva Guerra, an activist member of his human rights committee, who has been held since July 14 at a psychiatric hospital in Santiago de Cuba, on the island's southeast coast.

He said that Leyva, about 40, was given a series of six shock treatments shortly after being detained and hospitalized and another series of six in December. Afterward, Leyva reportedly was so disoriented that he did not even recognize his wife. The last treatment was so excessive, according to Sánchez, that it left Leyva with electrode burns on his temples.

"He isn't sick," Arcos declared. "they used these medical things to destroy his mind."

Sánchez noted that when human rights groups and Leyva's wife protested, the authorities responded that Leyva was "crazy" and that they were trying to cure him.

"We think when he leaves the hospital he will be worse," Sánchez said. Both Arcos and Sánchez displayed documents from Leyva's wife to support their charges.

A Cuban government official, asked to comment on the charges, responded by shrugging his shoulders and rolling his

124

eyes, then warned that it was dangerous for foreign journalists to interview the human rights dissidents without first advising the government.

A second case cited by Sánchez was undocumented, but he repeatedly stressed that it was authentic, based on interviews by monitors from his human rights group with another man who underwent the same treatment. He said the man, named Quesada, was released several months ago after being confined in one of two police-controlled pavilions at Havana's main psychiatric hospital.

"Before, he was completely sane," Sánchez said. "Now he is not the same man. In the psychiatric hospital he received massive electric shocks and psychoactive drugs." Psychoactive drugs, which are drugs designed to have a specific effect on the brain, could be used to tranquilize or otherwise alter prisoners' behavior.

'OUT OF CONTROL'

He said the hospital's two pavilions are under the strict control of the Interior Ministry, adding: "Usually the political police hospitalize dissidents in those pavilions. What occurs there is out of all democratic or humanitarian control."

With Sánchez during a recent interview was 24-year old José Luis Alvarado, who charged that he had been given shock treatments and heavy doses of psychoactive drugs in 1980 and 1982 at one of the pavilions while under sentence for attempting to leave Cuba.

"The first time I was given two sessions [of electric shock], and the second only one," Alvarado said. "I also had to take psychopharmic drugs three times daily, and so did the others.

125

There were about 100 prisoners in the pavilion. They used the psychiatric hospital to destroy the will of the person."

The two human rights officials described dozens of recent arrests, beatings and public clashes with police to underscore their belief that a new campaign against them is under way.

Attempts to silence the human rights groups eased in 1987 after Castro bowed to pressure from international human rights groups and a U.N. campaign led by the United States. He released hundreds of political prisoners and permitted leaders of the fledgling organizations to meet with visiting human rights workers, diplomats and journalists.

"Right now, there is more repression than in 1987 when the level — in terms of brutal violations of human rights — began to decline," Sánchez said. "Together with that decline came the flowering of the human rights groups, which continued until the arrival of the U.N. Human Rights Commission in September. During the visit, and above all after they left the country, there has been an increase in repression."

Sánchez and Arcos cited week by week chronologies of reported human rights violations during and since the U.N. Commission's visit. More than twenty persons were arrested during the visit for attempting to talk with U.N. investigators, they said, and at least ten of the eighty to one hundred people who were actually interviewed by the U.N. team were later arrested.

Since then, the rights leaders charged:

— Six artists and writers from a group favoring artistic freedom were beaten and arrested when they attempted to place flowers at a downtown Havana monument to José Martí, the 19th Century revolutionary poet revered as the father of Cuban Independence. Five

126

more members of the group, called Pro-Arte Libre, were later taken into custody.

— Two leaders of a political offshoot of Arcos' group, the Cuban Human Rights Party, also were jailed.

— Dozens of youths calling for greater freedom and more leisure activities for young people were attacked by plainclothes policemen when they marched through downtown Havana last Oct. 23. "It was almost a street battle," Arcos said, adding that all but one of thirty-six youths arrested that day were teenagers.

— In ensuing months, dozens more have been taken into custody and charged with civil offenses such as disorderly conduct for marching in demonstrations in at least three provinces outside the capital.

Although Cuba had charged such suspects with political crimes against the state until about two years ago, all the recent detainees have been sentenced or fined for civil offenses, Arcos and Sánchez said. This permits the government to deny that anyone is being held for political crimes, they charged.

As part of a long list of other rights abuses, Arcos accused a Havana policeman of murder in the shooting death of a 25-year old street salesman named Pedro Ortega Concha, who was peddling homemade plastic bottle caps, an illegal capitalist enterprise in Communist Cuba.

"The policeman asked him to hand over the bottle caps and, when he refused, shot him in the liver," Arcos said. "He died in a few minutes. The policeman is still working."

Despite the apparent rights crackdown, Cuba is meeting pledges made over the past year to release hundreds of political prisoners, according to American officials who monitor the situation here. They said that of the 450 prisoners Castro promised he would release, 250 are now free, most of them living as refugees in the United States. The promise was made last May to New York's Cardinal John J. O'Connor during the Roman Catholic prelate's visit to Cuba.

Cuban Rights, Even Today: Not So Libre

Joseph B. Treaster

Havana—In late October, a small group of Cubans working to improve human rights set out to lay a wreath at a monument to José Martí, the Cuban poet and independence hero, in a small park in the colonial section of Havana. Suddenly, they were assaulted by a mob of about fifty shouting, jeering men who witnesses say were plainclothes security police. Within minutes uniformed police arrived and arrested half a dozen of the human rights workers, charging them with creating a public disturbance. . . .

The leaders of Cuba's two main human rights groups cite this incident as an example of increased pressure and new tactics that the Government of Fidel Castro has been using against dissidents since a United Nations team looked into abuses of human tights here in mid-September. . . .

Elizardo Sánchez, the head of the Cuban Commission on Human Rights and National Reconciliation, said that at least thirty human rights workers have been arrested since the United Nations visit. Mr. Sánchez and Sebastián Arcos, a leader of the Cuban Committee on Human Rights, say another person active in human rights work, Jesús Leyva Guerra, has been confined to a psychiatric hospital since July and subjected to electric shock treatments. On a recent visit, Mr. Arcos said, Mr. Leyva, who has no history of mental illness, was unable to recognize his wife. . . .

Reprinted with permission from The New York Times, *19 January 1989. Copyright 1989 The New York Times Company.*

PSYCHIATRIC CONFINEMENT

MARY JANE CAMEJO

... Americas Watch is concerned about reports of the confinement of political prisoners in psychiatric hospitals, or the abuse of psychiatry by Cuban authorities to silence their opponents.

Nicolás Guillén Landrián, a former filmmaker, artist and poet, was expelled from ICAIC, the National Film Institute, in 1973 after his films were found to be "incoherent" or inconsistent with the goals of the revolution. One film, *Coffea Arábiga*, a 20-minute documentary on an agricultural plan implemented at the time, contained a scene in which Fidel Castro is seen climbing a mountain to the background soundtrack of the Beatles' *Fool on the Hill*. He had also refused to participate in an ICAIC film made in an effort to discredit Cuban writer Heberto Padilla who held "counterrevolutionary attitudes."

Guillen worked in a construction job until 1976 when he was arrested and accused of attempting to assassinate Castro. The charge was reportedly based on a comment he made at a social gathering. This charge was not pursued. However, he was held for six months without trial in the state security facility *Villa Marista*, and was interrogated but not physically abused. At his 1977 trial, he was sentenced to two years for "ideological diversionism."

During his imprisonment in Combinado del Este prison, he was taken to both the prison hospital and to the Havana Psychiatric Hospital and submitted to electric shock treatment. He was

130

later returned to Combinado del Este until his release. Guillen was released in 1979 only to be arrested six months later on two counts of "dangerousness". . . and served four more years. . . .

In July 1988, Jesús Leyva Guerra, a human rights activist, was detained and, at this writing, continues to be held in a psychiatric hospital in Santiago de Cuba. . . . Leyva is reported to have been subjected to a series [of] electric shock treatments, and was unable to recognize his wife on a recent visit.

Americas Watch has reason to believe Leyva has been confined to a psychiatric hospital as a reprisal for his human rights activity. Nevertheless, the details of his case remain unclear. If Leyva has been confined to treat any mental illness he may suffer, why has he been held in the judicial ward of the hospital? If he has been held in the judicial ward because he has criminal charges pending against him, what are they? If it is because he is considered by judicial authorities to be dangerous to himself or to society, has he actually caused harm to himself or to another person, or is this form of preventive detention?

While the abuse of psychiatry for political purposes is not known to be widespread in Cuba, Americas Watch has learned that a number of prisoners of conscience have been held in psychiatric hospitals during the initial period of detention, ostensibly to diagnose the prisoners' mental health. The following two prisoners of conscience recently released from Combinado del Este prison, were confined in the Havana Psychiatric Hospital upon arrest on charges of "enemy propaganda."

Ariel Hidalgo Guillén. . . spent the first twenty days of his detention in *Villa Marista*, and then was transferred to the psychiatric hospital. According to Hidalgo, he was held in a room with approximately one hundred criminally psychotic patients for ten days. No physicians or guards visited the ward during the time he was there. He had difficulty sleeping for fear of being attacked while he slept.

131

Julio Vento Roberes, a musician and cartoonist, was arrested in 1977 for drawing anti-government caricatures, and was reportedly confined in a psychiatric hospital for five years. Vento, who is 56 years old, began drawing cartoons again after his release. He was rearrested in 1982 and sentenced to eight years, again on charges of "enemy propaganda." Vento was previously imprisoned in 1960. . . .

Ex-Prisoner Found Hanged in Hospital

The former political prisoner Angel Tomás Quiñones, 39, apparently was found hanged, his body later incinerated by other patients in one of the security wards of the Havana Psychiatric Hospital, said Maria Reina Quiñones, the mother of the victim. During a press conference in Miami organized by a group of human rights activists led by Ricardo Bofill, Mrs Quiñones said that her son was not mentally ill and that she held the Cuban government responsible for his death. According to Mrs. Quiñones, her son spent a year in prison in 1972 accused of crimes against the integrity and stability of the nation and was a constant opponent of Fidel Castro.

Reprinted with permission from El Nuevo Herald (The Miami Herald*)*, *15 March 1990. Copyright 1990,* The Miami Herald.

FORENSIC PSYCHIATRY

AMNESTY INTERNATIONAL

... The Amnesty International visitors asked to visit the Havana Psychiatric Hospital because the organization had received occasional reports that political prisoners were taken there although it was not clear in what circumstances. Two wards had been mentioned in particular — the Sala Carbó-Serviá and the Sala Castellanos.

Amnesty International was told by officials that if certain behaviour is detected while a person is held in provisional detention or during the period leading up to the trial, s/he can receive a psychiatric examination either in the place of detention or, in the case of a serious problem, in a psychiatric hospital. First of all, a psychiatrist, psychologist and social worker go to visit the person in detention and if they think it necessary, the person is hospitalized. Prisoners already convicted can also be referred to a psychiatric hospital if they develop psychiatric problems while in prison. However, it was drawn to the attention of the visitors that in many cases the family of the detainee requested a psychiatric examination in order to determine whether extenuating circumstances of a psychiatric nature might be cited in their defence. The hospital has ten to thirty days to study the patient and to make a decision on how to proceed.

The Amnesty International visitors were permitted to visit the Sala Carbó-Serviá, which consisted of a poorly-lit main room with several rows of about ninety closely-packed beds, a

Reprinted with permission from Amnesty International, Cuba: Recent Developments Affecting the Situation of Political Prisoners and the Use of the Death Penalty, *pp. 24-25 (AI Index: AMR 25/04/88). Copyright 1988 Amnesty International.*

dining room with cement tables and benches, a sick bay, and several individual interviewing cubicles. The director of the unit explained that if an inmate showed signs of agitation, they would be taken to the sick bay, strapped to a bed and sedated. When asked if there was another ward in the hospital for forensic inmates, he said there was not. This was in contradiction with allegations made to Amnesty International by prisoners who say that while in the hospital, they were sent to a ward called Sala Castellanos as a form of punishment. Conditions there were described as very harsh.

Cases of prisoners known to Amnesty International to have spent time in the hospital were raised and the doctor provided detailed information from their files concerning the reasons why they had been taken there, how long they were kept there, what treatment they were given, and what diagnosis was made in each case. Amnesty International was later able to cross check some of this information with some of the prisoners concerned whom they interviewed in Combinado del Este Prison. One prisoner who told Amnesty International he was held in Sala Castellanos for 11 days in early 1987 said he was put in a punishment cell without a bed or mattress or toilet facilities. He had been taken there after trying to escape from Sala Carbó-Serviá.

Amnesty International has no reason to believe that political prisoners are referred for psychiatric tests for other than genuine forensic reasons. [**Editor's note:** *In December 1990, Amnesty International revised this assessment, stating that "Amnesty International fears that, in some cases, particularly political prisoners, the procedure [whereby individuals are confined to psychiatric institutions] may be open to abuse." For the complete December 1990 Amnesty statement, see pp. 181-183.*] However, people not suffering from any psychological disorder are held together with violent psychopaths and seriously disturbed people, making their stay there a very traumatic experience and leaving the practice open to abuse. The Sala Carbó-Serviá, an old dark building, contrasts starkly with the rest of the hospital premises, which are bright and modern. The Amnesty International visitors were told, however, that a brand new forensic psychiatry unit is being built where conditions and facilities would be considerably improved.

The Interrogation

Eugenio de Sosa Chabau

In 1977 I was a political prisoner at Combinado del Este Prison in Havana province. I already had been in prison for more than 17 years. One day I was suddenly called out of Combinado and taken to the State Security Headquarters in *Villa Marista* without being given a reason. . . . At *Villa Marista* I was interrogated repeatedly regarding some information I was supposed to have passed on to the "counterrevolutionary" exiles back in 1963! Their techniques to make me confess included constant threats that I was about to be shot; totally false assertions regarding incriminating testimony supposedly given by other prisoners — friends of mine — against me; isolation for days, naked, in a dark cell where I was supposed to lose track of day and night; involuntary administration of hallucinogenic drugs in the food (finally, when I found a semi-dissolved capsule in the food I stopped eating); being kept in an anechoic chamber (a "quiet" room with no echoes) for prolonged periods of time — where one could hear the sound of one's own bloodstream rushing and where the slightest sound is multiplied many times in intensity — and there subjected to extremely loud sounds at irregular intervals.

After my continued refusal to admit any sort of guilt or to incriminate my friends, they changed their tactics. I was in-

Reprinted from In a Place without a Soul: The Testimony of Former Cuban Political Prisoners, *pp. 9-10. Copyright 1985, The United States Information Agency.*

terviewed by a captain who, in a rather civilized manner, informed me that one of my daughters who lived in Texas had been allowed to come to Cuba to visit me with my granddaughters whom I had not yet met. This unusual move was granted, he told me, as a gesture of the Castro government before my execution for sending secret information to the enemies of the revolution a long time ago. My family, he told me, would come to Cuba by private jet.

After a few days, I was taken to the barber and given clean clothes in preparation for the first visit with my daughter in more than fifteen years. When I entered the room, instead of my daughter I found the same captain who, in a profound and grave tone, informed me that there was a terrible accident with the plane in which my family was coming and that my daughter and granddaughters were all dead. Months later I was to find out that the accident, as well as the visit arrangements, had all been fabrications of the torturers. But at that precise moment in Security Headquarters, when I was told of the "tragedy," I believed it. My reaction was swift: I jumped and punched the captain as hard as I could. I wanted to die. Needless to say, I immediately was beaten mercilessly by the guards. I was told that I would be shot the next day in La Cabaña fortress.

That night I was taken out of Security Headquarters and driven through Havana. At one point I was forced to lie down on the car. Soon we arrived at our real destination: the National Psychiatric Hospital.

The Psychiatric Hospital is one of the "jewels" of the revolution. It is a required stop for all foreign delegations that visit Cuba. The foreigners, of course, are not taken to the chamber of horrors where they put me, known as Carbó-Serviá Ward. There is another ward, called the Castellanos Ward, which is just as bad.

There were about eighty men in this ward, all violently disturbed. The smell of urine and excrement was sickening. There would be brawls among the patients every so often, and shattered, bloody bodies had to be carted out. During my stay, five patients were killed in brawls among themselves.

My first encounter with group electroshock treatments occurred one night when I saw a team of four men, directed by one called Mederos who was dressed as an orderly, enter the ward. Six patients were grabbed and rubber pieces stuffed into their mouths. They were thrown to the floor in a row side by side. Right there, on the floor, the electrodes were applied to both sides of the heads and the shocks applied. Six bodies started to contort one by one. The next six were then captured by the orderlies, forced to lie down and the procedure repeated. By then, the floor was already running with urine, excrement, and vomit. The shocks were applied to the temples of the patients, but to me they applied most of the shocks to the testicles instead. I received about fourteen electroshocks this way.

One day, some very young boys were brought into the ward. The oldest did not look older than 16. They had been caught writing anti-government graffiti on some building walls, and a "judge of the people" declared that to do such a thing they must be insane and in need of psychiatric treatment. Before the day was over all the boys were systematically gang-raped by more than thirty patients in the ward. To this day I can hear their cries for help and see their bloody bodies as I stood by in impotent rage. Not a single staff member intervened.

This nightmare, this terrible episode lasted for five months. It took place, I repeat, in 1977, in the 18th year of the revolutionary government of Cuba.

The Persistence of Darkness

Amaro Gómez Boix
Translated by Lilian Sotolongo Dorka

There's a place sealed in my thoughts and memories which, like monsters, is best kept secret. We never dare open that chest which keeps hidden the most abysmal of experiences that can never be forgotten. Sometimes, however, a captured memory escapes and lodges itself in the core of every thought, every word. It can happen even after ten years and three thousand miles have passed, when we find ourselves reclining leisurely on the terrace of a beautiful restaurant watching the vast ocean float by. This happened to me recently one evening at a beach in Southern California, when I was visited by the ghosts of *La Perrera* (the dog kennel).

IMMERSED IN THE ABSURD

Opening the door to my cell, the officer ordered, "648, pick up your belongings and come with me." I grabbed my towel and toothbrush and followed him. In an odd-looking room lay the clothes in which I had been arrested. After I dressed, the officer escorted me to a door at the rear of the building. I was handcuffed and put into a car.

This article originally appeared as a two part series. Part one is reprinted with permission from El Nuevo Herald (The Miami Herald), *10 February 1989; Part two is reprinted with permission from* El Nuevo Herald, *11 February 1989. Copyright 1989,* The Miami Herald.

Now there were three of us: the chauffeur, the officer sitting next to him, and me in the back seat. The streets of Havana seemed to race by either side of the speeding car. But I knew it was only an illusion. In reality, the city remained immobile, anchored in time for the past two decades.

I felt my heart leap as I was informed that I was to be subjected to a battery of tests in order to find out whether I was insane or whether my crime was a lesser one. "What type of tests? Who? How?" I didn't recognize the neighborhood we were passing, or the route, probably chosen to add yet another question mark to my consternation. Neither the officer nor the chauffeur said another word. Three Cubans sat silently in a car heading for somewhere. I had the ridiculous impression that the silence, although justified under the circumstances, was somehow exotic.

I really don't know how much more time went by. But before I knew it, we were on the grounds of the Havana Psychiatric Hospital, amidst well-kept gardens and light-colored pleasant-looking buildings.

In a kind of anteroom — half examination room and half office — a rather calm looking policeman disguised as a doctor ordered me to lower my pants. He then proceeded to examine my testicles. He then wrote something down on his notepad and asked me for my toothbrush. With uncharacteristic and unexpected distress, he broke the toothbrush in two close to the bristles. He threw the handle away and returned the other half to me. When you live in the absurd, events like that don't seem very surprising.

From there, I was taken to another section of the hospital where the doors had bars. An officer handed a document to a man with messy hair, grey skin and strange eyes. The officer left and the Grey Man ordered, "take off all of your clothes and put everything on that chair, including the shoes." After I had undressed, the Gray Man opened the barred door and led me into

140

a large open room filled with old worn-out cots. At the room's center was a corridor. At the end of the corridor there were iron bars with a doorway that led to a walled courtyard.

LA PERRERA

The large room was empty, but there, back in the courtyard, there were many. The Gray Man handed me a piece of soap and explained that I had to shower and then line up so I could be fumigated. So there I went, down the central corridor of my new home. My wardrobe consisted of a small towel, a piece of soap, and a mutilated toothbrush. As I walked toward the opening in the large iron bars, I thought to myself, "I must enter this place as if I were entering my own home." The tension in my muscles eased, and I kept myself from fueling the madness or fear of those there. I then entered the place where I would spend twelve hours per day, pitted against one hundred or so strangers. I had arrived at *La Perrera.*

La Perrera (the dog kennel) is the courtyard of the Carbó-Serviá ward of the Havana Psychiatric Hospital. It consists of 30 by 10 meter slabs of cement, bordered on one side by the wall of the ward and on the others by concrete barriers, each about fifteen to twenty feet high. Its roof is a latticework of iron bars with two wooden planks at the center. On the planks is perched a guard armed with an automatic rifle. Through the iron bars you can see a patchwork of sky and hear the songs of birds.

Newcomers to *La Perrera* must shower immediately upon arrival. Before they are issued a uniform, their genitals are fumigated with an atomizer. When night falls, sometime after we have our soup, it's time to line up close to one of the orderlies — mouth open, tongue extended. The orderly then places a five hundred milligram thorazine tablet on each tongue. As you close your mouth, you must in one motion place the pill between your lip

141

and gum with your tongue in order to avoid swallowing the pill. I had been warned, but the naive will swallow.

I once saw a tall, thin black man with enormous eyes plummet to the ground as if he had been shot dead on the spot. He was unlucky. He fell forward with all of his weight, hitting his teeth on a steel pipe. Bleeding profusely, he managed to beg for help between incomprehensible shouts of panic. But by that time, our phantom caretakers had retired, and there was no one around except the two soldiers on the roof of *La Perrera* and the soldier at the gate at the entrance of the ward. All we could do was give him some water and stick a handkerchief in his mouth. He howled like a wounded wolf, and not even the powerful pill that had thrown him down in the first place could mitigate his pain. By midnight, sleep finally overcame him. By morning, his sleep more resembled death.

Most of the inmates at Carbó-Serviá have deteriorated into a residue which was once life. Some have committed violent crimes and some are homicidal maniacs. They are men who aren't frightened by the stick or the whip. There are certain particularly subversive ones who think and survive in a world in which man should simply cease to exist. It is precisely the stubborn and non-submissive for which Carbó-Serviá is intended. The pavilion is only a small appendage of the prison system that reigns in Cuba. Everyone who serves time there either comes from another prison or from the old religious institution, *Villa Marista*, which has been converted by State Security into a sanctuary for their interrogations.

EL CAPÍTAN AND EL ENFERMERO

Mederos, who we call *El Enfermero*, the nurse, comes to us every morning. Mederos is a short, somewhat paunchy man who dresses in civilian clothes and wears a small, short-brimmed hat. Almost every day, his various assistants call out loudly the names of the unfortunate chosen who will be asked to lay down on the wet cement so that the electrical current will travel better. Mederos then fastens the electrodes and the entire process is performed with routine skill, which often entails overlooking the placement of a rubber bit in the prisoner's mouth. It is no surprise then, that when that first jolt of power zaps the prisoner's body, his teeth grind down on his tongue, turning his mouth into a bloodied foam.

Then there's *El Capítan*, the captain, the chief of the wing, who sodomizes the younger prisoners, threatening to turn them over to his two deranged bodyguards or to Mederos if they don't cooperate. *El Capítan* is a short, stubby man, with sallow skin and a frog-like mouth, who resembles [former Panamanian President] General [Manuel] Noriega a great deal. *El Capítan* hobbles about with great difficulty. Some say he was wounded when he took refuge in the Sierra Maestra under the orders of Juan Almeida, one of Castro's commanding officers. The less romantic simply say he was born bowlegged. What is known for sure is that *El Capítan* sexually abuses the younger prisoners. I can remember that after being raped, one young prisoner — who couldn't have been more than fourteen or fifteen years old — spent hours upon hours staring blankly, aimlessly into space, without ever really seeing.

NOTHING TO LOSE

"It was *El Capítan*," I was told by a veteran. I knew he wasn't lying, because men who have nothing left to lose don't lie. The Veteran was tall, thin and sad. He told me that Mederos would give him electroshock treatments every other day. He also told me that he had been at another prison before *La Perrera*. While there, another quite deranged prisoner had made

143

violent sexual threats. The Veteran defended himself by taking the other prisoner's eye out with a metal spoon.

"Now the guy has only one good eye left," he said to me, "but I'm here, and if I ever get out, I won't even recognize my own mother." He was an astonishingly lucid man who at that time could not have been more than thirty years old. I hope death looked upon him with mercy.

Life at *La Perrera* is non-stop from five in the morning until five in the evening, when it is time to eat the meager, clumpy meal. It is a routine existence, interrupted only by the arrival of a new prisoner, the most recent rape, or when some psychopath entertains himself by beating up another inmate.

I figured that I must have been at *La Perrera* for about two weeks when a policeman dressed as a sociologist asked me my name and the name of my mother and father. Having confirmed that my answers were correct, he smiled and took down some notes. I asked him if at any time they actually had doubted my sanity. "You never know," he said, and placed his note pad in his briefcase. I then asked him how much longer I would have to live there. "Not too much longer," he replied, "we're almost finished."

DESTINY OF THE NON-SUBMISSIVE

Later, I was interviewed by another, younger man, who appeared to be more intelligent. He insinuated that soon I would be taken back to *Villa Marista*.

"You've seen that the conditions here are not the best. It wouldn't be very good for you if you had to come back here. You've really got to have a lot of courage to come back here, Amaro." He pronounced my name with reflective anxiety. Two or three days later, he came to take me away.

Yes, as it is for most people, there is a place in my memory which has been sealed off. But the Carbó-Serviá ward of the Havana Psychiatric Hospital remains open, with *La Perrera* anxiously awaiting the stubborn and the non-submissive.

PSYCHIATRY AND POLITICS IN CUBA

ROBERTO VALERO

TRANSLATED BY RICHARD O'CONNELL, JR.

In October of 1980, I met the famous Russian writer Vladimir Bukovsky in Caracas. We talked, half in Russian and half in English, about the technical advances made by Russian and Cuban-Russian psychiatry. Although we could speak neither of the two languages fluently, we could communicate, since both Mr. Bukovsky and I were surprised to have lived in almost the same place as far as our psychiatric experiences go.

Vladimir Bukovsky suffered in the Soviet Union from a new disease discovered by Soviet doctors called "opposition." In his statements to the Caracas press on the 19th of October [1980], Bukovsky explained the direct and scientific relationship between the KGB and medical personnel in Soviet mental hospitals.

The Cuban government, jealous that the motherland might get ahead, prepared a magnificent program for its dissidents, very similar to and in some cases better than the Soviet model.

I remember vividly my friend Juan Peñate Fernández, who studied classical languages and history at the University of Havana with a profound knowledge of philosophy, music and politics. On the eve of the World Festival of Youth and Students (1978), Peñate decided to come down with "opposition." Peñate suffered from a terrible illness in his eyes that was so advanced, he almost lost the use of his vision. He went to see Dr. Orfilio Peláez, who swore that he could not authorize the needed operation, which was available to Cubans only in the Soviet Union or in [East] Germany, unless the illness became more serious (blindness in both eyes, for example).

Furious and terribly depressed, Peñate returned home and discussed the situation with a cousin. In his kitchen, he yelled that the Cuban authorities were crazy if they thought that he was going to ask for asylum in the Soviet Union, as it was even worse than Cuba. At the time, Peñate did not know that his neighbor, a disciplined and perfectly moral Socialist and president of the local Committee for the Defense of the Revolution, had heard everything.

The next day, two gentlemen dressed in civilian clothing presented themselves at Peñate's home and asked him to accompany them. They promised Mr. Peñate's parents that their son would return home that afternoon.

He was taken to the police station in Vedado (21st and C Streets in Havana) and put him in prison without telling him why. When it came time for dinner, they spit in his food. That night at Combinado del Este Prison, he was stripped, dressed in white, and taken to the National Psychiatric Hospital, also known as Mazorra.

The "doctors" and "nurses" in Mazorra used a variety of methods: isolation; confinement with murderers, rapists and schizophrenics; ice-cold baths at five in the morning; and drugs which increased the pressure in his eyes (when he refused to take the drugs, they were force fed to him through beatings).

One nurse was an old pederast who asked inmates to sleep with him. If they refused, their names would appear on a list for electroshock treatments the following morning. There were individuals who had spent twenty years there without receiving either correspondence or visits.

Of course, Peñate attempted suicide without success. You can live for a couple of days in total incomprehension, but when

147

it is for twenty days, a month, or forty days — and without any-one bothering to explain why you are there, you conclude that you are asleep and that you should kill yourself. It is better than living because you cannot accept a system — regardless of how monstrous it is — could have a ward like this one in the middle of the capital, the Mederos ward of the Havana Psychiatric Hospital.

Forty-eight days later Peñate was taken to the entrance of the hospital. They returned his money and his clothes, and told him to go home. He was cured. He had his certificate of discharge in his shirt pocket. They had cured him.

He arrived a couple of days later back at his job. His boss did not say anything, not even asking him where he had been.

The next two years (1979-1980) were very difficult for Peñate. He received more than twenty phone calls and numerous visits from State Security agents asking him to cooperate with them. In other words they wanted him to become an agent. The State Security agents never mentioned blackmail, nor what had happened in the hospital.

At the end of 1979, Peñate participated in a series of writers' meetings. Among those participating were the novelist Reynaldo Arenas, Vicente Echerri, and others who had not incorporated themselves into the official culture and therefore could not publish.

State Security asked Peñate to sign an accusation against me for having incited him to "counterrevolutionary work and leave the country illegally."

. . .Of course, they did not mention the medical incident. My friend came to Matanzas to tell me the bad news. A terrible blow was being prepared against me because I too had succumbed to the virus of opposition in July 1979 when I went to the Agence France Presse to denounce the blackmail to which I was being subjected. As a friend of numerous political prisoners and dissident writers who refused to take part in the government's literary carnivals, I was very "sick."

On the fifth of February I suffered a setback. I was expelled from the University of Havana. I did not ask for clemency. I did not applaud and I did not cry. I went to Peñate's house and we met up with Reynaldo Arenas. We had to leave in a little boat.

On the 22nd of March we were detained and I was released on the condition that I stayed at home. On the 5th of April, my friend Peñate and I succeeded in getting by the police barriers and the walls of the Peruvian Embassy.

Peñate fled to Spain, but not before being subjected to the crowds throwing sticks and stones at him. We were marked like publicly condemned men. When he left the Peruvian Embassy, Peñate called Dr. Orfilio Peláez to tell him that he could not see very well and that he needed medical attention. The good doctor, an example of "the new Socialist Man" said that he did not treat worms.

Today Peñate lives in Madrid. He is very poor but lives without the fear of someone spitting in his food. He is very sick with both an eye disease and throat cancer. He lives alone and sad, but without fear that people are listening behind doors. I sent this article to him as a greeting and to you the readers as a notice: a small effort to counteract totalitarian psychiatry.

A Cuban's Testimony

By Juan Peñate Fernández
Translated by Richard O'Connell, Jr.

. . . Roberto Valero tells of some of my most painful memories of being forcibly interned in 1978 at the Havana Psychiatric Hospital. Regrettably, Valero made some errors. . . . Among the installations of this type on the island I am intimately familiar with Mazorra, a hospital with a long and sad history. . . .

Valero talks about a "Mederos ward." It does not exist. Mederos is the last name of a male orderly (who actually is a functionary of Cuban State Security) who is in charge of the wards named Castellanos and Carbó-Serviá. . . . Foreign visitors to the Havana Psychiatric Hospital should be familiar with the Paredes ward, the best ward in the hospital, with its lustrous, meticulously polished floors. The visitor will be told about the progress made by a few rehabilitated prisoners while he walks through the well-groomed gardens of the model hospital, listening to various official statistics. . . .

But they [the staff at the hospital]. . . do not take guests through the cells of the Castellanos or Carbó-Serviá pavilions. . . . In these two wards, [political prisoners] survive like dogs among madmen. . . . They are not sick; they display no pathology except dissent against the Castro regime and its manner of building communism; dissent which, in Cuba, is called pathological. . . .

These wards are filthy black holes. They are places where prisoners are transferred after being held for days in tiny cells at Combinado del Este prison in order to make them manageable and subdued through irresponsible applications of electroshock administered without reliable medical supervision. They are wards in which the fantastic and the uniquely evil are joined; common thieves, murderers and political prisoners all come together. Someone who sought asylum in a Latin American embassy survives next to criminals. . . . All are watched by threatening guards who show off their weapons from their perch on top of the fence circling the yard.

It is also common that the drugs administered as medicine are the same for everyone. Very early in the morning, those named on a list for treatment are given electroshocks on floors still wet from the morning cleaning.

Valero says that I tried to kill myself. Except as a point of personal clarification, it is not very important to contradict this false rumor circulated about me. . . . I say that it is not important because we all were obsessed with death in that place. Although I did not try to kill myself, we all thought about it.

I remember a boy who tried to get asylum in the Venezuelan Embassy. He wanted them to apply electroshocks and each time with increasing force so that he could be declared insane at the moment of his trial. I also remember a prisoner who asked them to let him die after receiving a horrible beating in the yard of the Carbó-Serviá ward.

Because of these things. . . I plead that the public see my corrections and with them my protest against a brutal system of arbitrary detentions as practiced in Cuba.

151

Statement by Mrs. Juana Josefina Garrido Ojeda to the U.N. Commission on Human Rights Havana, 1 November 1988

Translated by Armando Lago

Through this denunciation, Mrs. Juana Josefina Garrido Ojeda, born 24 November 1942, unemployed, and resident of Presneda No. 209, First Floor, between Millar and Recreo Streets, Regla, Havana, wishes to inform the United Nations Commission on Human Rights that her son, Manuel Tejera Garrido, has been detained at Combinado del Este Prison since 21 August [1988], accused of illegal exit from the country after having been captured at sea twenty-two miles from the Cuban coast. He has not yet been brought to trial. Mrs. Garrido states that her 21 year-old son always has been opposed to the political system in Cuba, a fact that appears in the official file on his case at State Security. The same file describes him as "apathetic to socialist society." Because of this characterization, he was committed to the Carbó-Serviá psychiatric ward for one week and then released after being diagnosed as "apathetic to socialism." Mrs. Garrido adds that Manuel, who attempted to leave Cuba in a primitive raft along with six of his friends, told her before making his decision to leave Cuba that he "would rather be eaten by sharks than continue living under Castro's regime."

Mrs. Garrido is grieving because on 1 September [1988], another of her four sons, a nineteen year-old suffering from asthma, died during an operation for an injured arm as a result of an overdose of anesthesia. She also states that another son, Francisco Tejera Garrido, is confined to the Naval Hospital in the psychiatric ward. The authorities have told her that he will not be released until he serves a sentence equal to his military service obligation. Francisco, who is confined to Ward G, Third Floor, Bed 17, also opposes the regime. He prefers remaining confined, diagnosed as insane, to returning to military training and being sent to Angola. He was interned on 5 September of this year [1988].

Mrs. Garrido also notes that since 19 March 1988, Manuel Tejera Garrido has been a member of the Cuban Committee for Human Rights (*Comité Cubano Pro Derechos Humanos*) headed by Dr. Ricardo Bofill Pages and has participated in a number of the diverse activities undertaken by this pacifist and humanitarian organization.

(signed)

Juana Josefina Garrido Ojeda
Identification Card #42112401831

Tania Díaz Castro
Secretary General
Partido Pro Derechos Humanos

Dr. Samuel Martínez Lara
Executive Secretary
Partido Pro Derechos Humanos

Marcelo Vera Mellado
Member
Partido Pro Derechos Humanos

153

The Mind of a Prisoner: The Case of an Exiled Activist Fuels Charges of Abuse in Cuban Psychiatric Hospitals

Liz Balmaseda

Jesús Leyva Guerra says he doesn't remember the worst that happened to him the last time he was in the Gustavo Machín psychiatric hospital in Santiago de Cuba.

After six days of electric shock treatments and heavy doses of psychoactive drugs, he was so disoriented he didn't recognize his wife. Oblivious to her presence in the visitors' hall, he sat down at another table with strangers.

Elba Leyva recalls that her husband's arms and legs were swollen, and his temples had electrode burns. "He was out of it, like a drunk, dead gone. He would drool all over himself," she says.

This was last fall, the last time Leyva — a 42-year old human rights activist and political dissident — was in a Cuban psychiatric ward. The story of his detention in Cuban hospitals for what he alleges were political reasons has ignited charges that the Cuban government has been using psychiatric abuse to silence dissidents.

"They wanted to make me crazy," says Leyva, now living in Miami Beach.

The campaign against the alleged abuses has attracted support beyond the usual activist groups in and out of Cuba. Both the American Psychiatric Association and U.S. Sen. Claiborne Pell, D-RI, have asked for investigations in Leyva's case.

Other protests have cited the cases of Julio Soto Angurel, a human rights activist held in Havana's national psychiatric hospital, and Orlando Polo, an environmentalist and dissident who was released from that hospital Oct. 13 after 21 days.

Although former prisoners and patients say such abuses have been going on for years, these are relatively new charges against Cuba, where human rights criticism has centered mostly on the imprisonment of the government's political opponents.

Cuba has denied the latest allegations.

Leyva, who left Cuba on a special U.S. visa granted to Cuban political prisoners, arrived in Miami earlier this month.

He says his troubles began during the early 1970s. A merchant marine active in his workers' union, he took up the cause of shipmates who complained about unsafe working conditions. His labor activism, Leyva says, soon led to clandestine dissident activities. Beginning in 1978, he was arrested several times and held at both the Santiago psychiatric hospital and Havana's national psychiatric hospital, known as Mazorra. Cuban human rights activists claim Mazorra's judicial wards are controlled by the Ministry of Interior.

In 1983, doctors declared Leyva a paranoid schizophrenic, and he was forced into electric shock treatment for the first time, he says.

Such treatments, which induce seizures, often are effectively used for patients suffering from severe depression, says Miami psychiatrist Rolando Fernandez.

POLITICAL ARRESTS

But Leyva says the doctors who evaluated him always asked his political views. And human rights observers say his arrests were clearly political.

In November 1987, for instance, he was arrested moments after leaving the home of Elizardo Sánchez, a prominent human rights activist now in prison. He was most recently detained in July 1988 for doing work for a human rights organization. He says he was taken by force to the Santiago hospital, where he promptly began a hunger strike. On the sixth day of his hunger strike, he says, he was given the first of six electric shock treatments. "Later, they told me I ate on the eighth day of my hunger strike, but I don't remember," says Leyva, who is undergoing a voluntary psychiatric evaluation in Miami. He hopes to prove the Cubans' diagnosis of paranoid schizophrenia wrong. The soft-spoken Leyva talks about his imprisonments as if reciting someone else's biography. He describes the alleged abuses in objective detail. Although he is relieved to be out of Cuba, he says the past is not behind him.

These days, he worries about finding an inexpensive apartment for himself, his wife, and three young children and fitting interviews with journalists and human rights groups in his schedule.

"DIVERSE APPLICATIONS"

Cuban officials have touted their use of psychology in law enforcement. Speaking to Cuban psychologists in March 1987, recently ousted Interior Minister José Abrantes said that his ministry had "the most diverse, universal, and decisive application" of psychology in Cuba.

The most recent allegations of abuse are "simply a political campaign," says Julio Espinosa, an official at the Cuban Interests Section in Washington. "Where is their proof? I am convinced that in Cuba no one is tortured. Everyone knows how advanced Cuba is in the field of medicine and that Mazorra is an excellent facility."

However, a Minnesota clinical psychologist who specializes in treating tortured victims calls the Cubans' methods "suspicious." "I would find any results of any such medical evaluations [under these circumstances] to be suspicious," says Rosa Garcia-Peltoniemi, research coordinator in Minneapolis at the Center for Victims of Torture.

Of Human Rights, a Washington-based group that campaigns against abuses in Cuba, launched a drive in January to free Leyva, distributing 10,000 fliers to American psychiatrists, urging them to write protest letters to Fidel Castro.

OTHER INQUIRIES

There were other inquiries. Rhode Island Sen. Pell had met with Castro five months earlier and in March, asked the Cuban leader to probe the Leyva case. And the American Psychiatric Association's committee on human rights wrote to Cuba's chief of psychiatry for the public health ministry.

"It is our sincere hope that this is not happening in Cuba," wrote the committee's chairman, Dr. Lawrence Hartmann.

But the allegations are difficult to investigate. The World Psychiatric Association will not get involved because Cuba is not a member country.

Cuba joined the Soviet Union, Czechoslovakia and Bulgaria in dropping out of the association in protest of its moves to expel the Soviets for psychiatric abuse in 1983. This year, the Soviets were readmitted after reforms were reported.

"The Cubans have adopted the Soviet model across the board. I'm not surprised they are also using psychiatry the way the Soviets used to," says Of Human Rights director Frank Calzon.

SIMILAR STORIES

Like Leyva's story, other Mazorra cases are surfacing.

The international human rights group America's Watch has noted the case of dissident artist and filmmaker Nicolás Guillén Landrián, who it says fell from grace during the early 1970s, when one of his films depicted Castro climbing a mountain to the tune of the Beatles' *Fool on the Hill.* Guillén was arrested in 1976 and given electric shock treatments in Mazorra. He later was released and is a human rights activist in Havana.

Perhaps the most poignant tale is that of Amaro Gómez Boix, a Cuban writer now living in California, who was once a patient in Mazorra. Writing in *El Nuevo Herald* [*The Miami Herald*] earlier this year, he described some of the hospital's infamous characters, including one they called "the nurse."

"Each day his various assistants call out loudly the names of the unfortunate chosen who will be asked to lie down on the wet cement so that the electrical current will travel better," wrote Gomez.

"[He] then fastens the electrodes, and the entire process is performed carelessly, which often entails overlooking the placement of a rubber guard in the prisoners mouth. It's no surprise then, that when the first jolt of power zaps the prisoners body, his teeth grind down on his tongue, turning his mouth into a bloody foam."

TESTING CUBA'S LIMITS: ONE DISSIDENT'S QUEST FOR FREE EXPRESSION

GEORGE GEDDA

All criticism is opposition.
All opposition is counter-revolutionary.
— Fidel Castro

That demanding standard would appear to leave Cubans who are disenchanted with their system little choice but to remain silent or to head for the more congenial confines of Miami. But Roberto Bahamonde is a different breed of dissident. He won't leave Cuba and he won't keep quiet about what he regards as the serious shortcomings of the Cuban revolution. His persistent questioning of Castro's doctrine has kept him in trouble with the law for much of his adult life. He has spent more than two years in detention, including extended periods in a psychiatric hospital where he claimed he was subjected to electric shock treatments administered not by a doctor but by a torture expert. Now 54, he is a political prisoner once again.

He is one of many victims of what the State Department and private human rights groups regard as a significant increase in political repression in Cuba over the past year and a half. The crackdown reflects the uneasiness of a regime that suddenly finds itself ideologically isolated and uncertain about future assistance from the Soviet Union. Still, Castro retains a strong core of support and, with dissidents such as Bahamonde either in jail or intimidated, his hold on power seems secure, at least for the short term. In March 1989, Bahamonde entered the race for a municipal assembly seat from his neighborhood district in the outskirts of Havana, running as an advocate of free enterprise, free speech, establishment of a multi-party system, free emigration, and a free press. That he lost this quixotic quest was no surprise. What did raise eyebrows was that a dissident would try to use the electoral process as a vehicle for change in Cuba's Marxist-Leninist state. There are no known precedents in 31 years of Castro's rule for what Bahamonde did in March 1989. It was a classic match-up: Bahamonde, the pro-capitalist insurgent, against a veteran of the Angola war known for his unswerving support of the revolution.

Although Bahamonde lost, he reinforced in a unique way the widespread notion that some Cubans would welcome the kind of change he advocates. His efforts also provide a rare insight into the way Cuban authorities deal with renegades like Bahamonde. While multi-candidate elections were instituted years ago, a variety of mechanisms have been introduced to ensure that only the party faithful prevail and that less than resolute supporters of the regime remain on the periphery.

ENFORCING CONFORMITY

For much of the time since the municipal election, life for Bahamonde has been a horror story, beginning with a pre-dawn knock at the door by the political police two weeks after his election night adventure. The crackdown against him was probably less the product of his bid for office as a regime critic than other manifestations of his nonconformity. He is, after all,

160

a member of the Cuban Commission on Human Rights and National Reconciliation, one of several independent, unauthorized groups that tried to make a political statement in April 1989 during the visit to Havana of Soviet President Mikhail Gorbachev. Bahamonde and twenty of his friends were arrested about thirty-six hours after Gorbachev's arrival, presumably because they were planning to take part in a pro-Gorbachev demonstration at the Soviet embassy the night before the Kremlin leader's departure. The dissidents want for Cuba the kinds of reforms Gorbachev has instituted in the Soviet Union. After the arrests, the demonstration was canceled, but police maintained a strong presence outside the embassy to guard against unexpected developments.

Three days later, with no defense attorney present, Bahamonde was convicted in a closed trial on charges of attending illegal meetings. So far as is known, only two of his colleagues who were arrested at the time of Gorbachev's visit also remain in detention, but other human rights activists have been convicted and sentenced since then on what appear to be politically motivated grounds. After his arrest, Bahamonde said he was told that his problems arose partly from a lengthy interview he granted to me on March 31 at his home. Sentenced to three months in prison, he was taken to Combinado del Este prison in Matanzas, about seventy miles east of Havana.

A few weeks after he began serving his sentence, Cuban authorities dealt him an even more damaging blow: he was tried and convicted on a charge of working as a free-lance photographer without a license. His three-month prison term was extended by one year. The timing of the government action left the clear impression that he was being penalized for his political activities. Cuba is filled with moonlighters who, although ostensibly required to have a license, operate without one. If they are non-political, the government normally looks the other way.

This has been an especially trying time for family members because of Bahamonde's prison conditions. His wife, Rafaela, said after a New Year's eve visit that the cell Bahamonde shares with seven other inmates had been fouled by human waste that dripped down through the ceiling for the previous month. He had suffered a dangerous weight loss and complained that his rations were becoming increasingly smaller and less appetizing. Early this year, both prison conditions and his health improved.

Bahamonde's experience illustrates once again the strict — at least by Western Standards — constraints on both personal and political freedom in Cuba. There are official guidelines for personal behavior, both written and unwritten, which most Cubans choose not to challenge. Yet the rules governing limitations on free speech are somewhat more free than is widely believed abroad. In contrast to the situation a generation ago, Cubans can be remarkably candid in private conversations, depending on the circumstances. One Cuban went so far as to admit to me in the presence of a government official that he had seen an American-made anti-Castro documentary that had been smuggled onto the island. Thousands of Cubans listen to the U.S. government's Radio Martí with no apparent penalty, although the station's more irrepressible listeners may possibly find themselves at the bottom of the list for benefits such as a new apartment or a college education. Countless Cubans attend church services. There is far more religious tolerance in Cuba than, say in many Muslim countries. And while churchgoers are never invited to become party members, they probably do not have to worry about losing their jobs.

In some Latin American countries, dissidents like Bahamonde routinely are gunned down by death squads. Bahamonde, although a police target for years, had been able to earn a living before his most recent arrest and to raise a family. He and Rafaela have four children ranging in age from 17 to 24. His oldest child, Roberto, had difficulty gaining admission to the university because of his father's irreverent attitude toward the revolution, but the authorities eventually relented; Roberto graduated in 1989 with a degree in engineering and now has a job.

HISTORY OF DISSENT

Bahamonde is a pleasant man with a baritone voice and the sort of diction associated with a well ordered mind. One night last year a few days before his arrest, Bahamonde spoke to this reporter about the indignities he had suffered as one who refuses to accept things as they are under Castro. He first ran afoul of the law in 1971 when he wrote a letter to Castro encouraging abandoning moral incentives for workers in favor of material incentives. He believed only higher pay could stimulate an increase in Cuba's lagging production. The letter earned Bahamonde a nineteen-day detention, the last four days of which were spent at a psychiatric hospital outside Havana. He was sent home with a certificate stating that he was suffering from paranoia.

His most traumatic experience with the authorities began on May 27, 1975, when, while working at a state cattle farm, he was accused of attempting to instill fellow workers with anti-regime sentiments. After twenty days imprisonment, Bahamonde was sent back to the psychiatric hospital. There he came under the sadistic control of one Heriberto Madeiros [sic], who was in charge of administering electric shock treatments. Bahamonde matter-of-factly described Madeiros's methodology. "He did them (the treatments) without doctors' ordering them," he said, adding that he suffered afterward from hypersensitivity and loss of memory. "It took me years to recover. I recognized my family, but there were friends whose names I did not remember. But little by little I got my memory back. I think now I'm all right. I feel good."

His imprisonment lasted 10 months, until March 1976, but in January 1983, he was arrested once again and sent back to the psychiatric hospital. Bahamonde is able to discuss his various imprisonments, but Rafaela cannot; she makes no effort to hide her bitterness about the cruelty to which her husband has been subjected. She spoke of his experience in the hospital's "punishment wing" — beatings, madmen wandering around naked, deaths resulting from shock treatment, and confinement cells laced with excrement. "I felt like throwing up," she said. "I had to see him there amid all the stench." He was detained for 56 days and released without explanation.

After his 1983 release, Bahamonde was not permitted by the government to work in his profession as an agricultural engineer. He earned what he could working as a free-lance photographer, even though the authorities refused to give him the license required of all who are self-employed in Cuba.

In March 1989, when the municipal assembly elections were held, Bahamonde saw an opportunity to make political points. The local election in his neighborhood, a somewhat rundown area in east Havana known as San Miguel de Padron, was set for March 9. Political campaigning in Cuba is forbidden; voters make their choices based on biographical data about the candidates. (Castro looks with disdain on U.S.-style elections, arguing that candidates make extravagant promises during the campaign, then break them after their election.) But Bahamonde made his intentions known to some of his neighbors, explaining what he stood for.

Not many voters ventured out on that chill, rainy evening, but there was a large police presence, part of a not-so-subtle effort to discourage potential votes for Bahamonde. As additional insurance, the party militant in charge of the proceeding recommended the election of Geraldo Aldama, the establishment candidate, and he refused Bahamonde permission to speak. The election was held, Bahamonde's opponent won the show-of-hands vote (there was no vote count), and that seemed to be the end of it. But Bahamonde maintained that the refusal to allow him to speak was a procedural error. He appealed to the municipal electoral council for a new election. Surprisingly, the appeal was upheld, and the citizens of San Miguel de Padron reconvened on the night of March 20, again with the police looking on. Once again, however, Bahamonde was denied permission to read his platform. The session turned into a sometimes acrimonious debate over Bahamonde's past troubles with the law.

Bahamonde's critics seized on the rumors that he had once plotted an attempt on Castro's life and that he had tried to leave the country during the Mariel boat lift of 1980, an allegation that he vigorously denies. (Neighborhood militants wanted to expel him aboard the boatlift, but for unexplained reasons, government officials insisted that he remain in Cuba.) To put to rest that recurring charge, Bahamonde obtained a letter from the Immigration Ministry confirming that he had never attempted to flee the country. The issue was potentially crucial since the government has systematically attempted to portray those who left from Mariel in 1980 as traitors and "scum."

Bahamonde's credentials as a candidate were reviewed for more than an hour of often heated debate before the assembly chairman called for a vote count, which was agreed to. The final tally was 31 for Bahamonde, 60 for his opponent, and 59 abstentions. Bahamonde believed not illogically that most who abstained sympathized with his views. He read their abstention as a protest vote. After the March 20 balloting, Bahamonde once again asked for a new election, contending that he was improperly denied permission to read his platform to his neighbors. He lodged his appeal with the state electoral council, which on April 1, 1989 ruled against him. Bahamonde's arrest on April 4 seemed related more to the protest activities he had planned during the Gorbachev visit than to his electoral ambitions. If Cuban authorities were genuinely disturbed by the prospect of a pro-free speech capitalist making headway through the electoral system, then Bahamonde probably would have been picked up at the time of his candidacy rather than during Gorbachev's stay.

What apparently struck fear in the hearts of the authorities was the specter of Gorbachev's visit being used by Bahamonde and other dissidents to rally opposition to Castro. Indeed, many Cubans see Gorbachev as their best hope for an eventual political relaxation in Cuba and an improvement in living standards. Cubans used to await eagerly Spanish-Language Soviet publications, until the summer of 1989, when Castro banned them for their sometimes sneering attitude toward socialism.

Bahamonde's experience as a candidate underscored another profound difference between Cuba and the Soviet Union these days: less than a week before Bahamonde made his electoral bid, national elections were held in the Soviet Union after a campaign in which, unlike Cuba, public policy issues were the subject of extended debate. The results indicated strong backing for Gorbachev's reform program. The refusal to allow Bahamonde permission to state publicly his views before a neighborhood gathering is but one illustration of how far the Soviets have drifted ideologically from Cuba under Gorbachev's tutelage.

But Eastern Europe is moving resolutely on the democratic path, and it must have been extraordinarily unsettling for Castro to see one ally after another in that region toppled in the latter half of 1989. But so long as Castro remains wedded to his orthodox approach to socialism, Gorbachev's admirers in Cuba are well advised to keep to themselves. Bahamonde chose not to and is paying a steep price. He'll be behind bars until July. [*Editor's note:* Bahamonde was released in July of 1990.]

My Personal Testimony on Psychiatric Abuse in Cuba

Ariel Hidalgo Guillén

My name is Ariel Hidalgo. I graduated with a B.A. in history and was a high school teacher of Marxist philosophy and political economy. I am also the author of *Origins of the Workers Movement and Socialist Thinking in Cuba* which has been included in the bibliography of humanities at the university level in Cuba. On the 19th of August 1981, because of my disapproval of the Cuban government's organized repudiation of those who left via the port of Mariel in 1980 (a position which cost me my teaching post), State Security agents searched my house. After their search, I was taken to Havana's Center of Security Investigations, better known among Cubans as *Villa Marista,* where they accused me of "enemy propaganda." The basis for this charge was, among other things, my collaboration on a manuscript which was a leftist critical analysis of the social system ruling Cuba entitled *Cuba: The Marxist State and the New Class.*

On the 9th of September, after twenty days of interrogation, I was handcuffed, placed in a car and driven to what at the time was an unknown destination: the Havana Psychiatric Hospital.

I was placed in an area closed off with iron bars which I later found out was called Sala Carbó-Serviá. Upon seeing the inhuman expressions of the inmates, my first impression was that I was entering a cage of gorillas. Once inside, I realized that I was at the complete mercy of a hundred men — convicts from different prisons, the overwhelming majority of whom were violently insane. Among them were murderers and rapists.

168

The doctors never crossed the shadows of the bars, and the orderlies only entered when they had to remove someone forcibly to be subjected to electroshock treatment.

From sunrise to sunset, a group of leaders, self-appointed by use of force, made the majority of the inmates stay outside on a small patio six meters long enclosed only by iron bars and offering no shade from the sun. The worst part of this, however, was not the lack of protection from the elements. It was having to share such a small space with eighty or ninety psychotic people. During that time, I had to stand, not only because of the lack of space, but also because the floor was covered with excrement, saliva, sperm, et cetera. The most repulsive acts imaginable took place there, including rapes and beatings of defenseless elderly persons.

They only let us enter for a few minutes to eat. Shortly before meal time, dozens of people would push for the door and upon its opening a deafeningly loud horde would descend upon the two large tables in a space within Sala Carbó-Serviá designated as the dining room. When you entered, the food already was on the tables. Plates were so close together to one another, that people had to climb on top of each other in order to eat. The surge of people entering immediately made everything even worse. Some inmates got two or three plates; the strong took the food away from the weak. Some, in their desperation to get one or two rations to eat, ran on top of the tables, stepping on plates or knocking them on the ground. If I succeeded in getting a plate of food I had to eat surrounded by insane people. Because of the savagery of my neighbors, it was an effort to keep the food down.

At night, I could barely close my eyes for fear that some maniac would try and take advantage of my sleep to commit some outrageous act. Lighting on fire the socks of sleeping prisoners was one of the principal ways to pass the time. Some of the more deranged prisoners masturbated and urinated on those who slept.

I was kept there for ten days during which I was taken out of the ward on only one occasion. It was for half an hour, during which I was given a psychiatric evaluation. Looking back on it, if someone killed me in one of those violent disagreements which were so common, I think my murder would have gone unpunished.

As an additional anecdote, I would like to add that after five days in the Sala, a sane young man was added to our number. I say sane because of the expression of terror on his face upon entering, which, I imagine, was similar to that on mine when I arrived. He sat down by the bars next to the entrance and, like an ostrich burying its head in the sand, hid his head in his folded arms. I asked him about himself. He told me that he was a pediatrician named José Arturo García (I think he is already in the United States) and that because of a few words said to a girl friend in jest, was charged with planning the murder of President Fidel Castro.

Since there were no beds available, I gave him my mattress to sleep on, and slept on the frame. After talking to him for a long while (he calmed down when realized that he was not alone in his sanity) he confessed, "If you had not spoken to me, I would have killed myself."

(signed)

Ariel Hidalgo (Guillén)

Psychiatric Abuse in Cuba

Transcript of a WLTV-TV Channel 23 news-series prepared and narrated by Lourdes Meluza. Transcription and translation by Alice Martinez

Ariel Hidalgo: He told me that I was crazy — hopelessly crazy.

Eduardo Martínez: We were going through Rancho Bolleros Avenue and I asked myself, "Where are they taking me now?

Andrés Solares: They told me that if I insisted on not talking and not telling the names of my friends, they would put me in Mazorra with all of the insane people.

Lourdes Meluza: This is Mazorra, Havana's psychiatric hospital and Cuba's showcase of advances in health care. This model hospital has wards unknown to visitors, where the Dante-esque nightmare of pre-revolutionary Mazorra has not ended. A nightmare not forgotten by Cuban dissidents now living in Miami. . . .

Eduardo Martínez: (caption notes that he was sent to Mazorra in 1981 for counter-revolutionary activities) The ward is called Carbó-Serviá. There were

	rapists, mentally ill people. There were chronic cases, and one had to live with those people.
Andrés Solares:	(caption notes that he was sent to Mazorra in 1981 for founding a political party) We saw crazy people hit each other. There were people in crisis thrown into a yard alone, so that they could hit themselves against the floor.
Lourdes Meluza:	The hospital is five minutes from Rancho Bolleros International Airport. There are four thousand mentally ill individuals living within sixty-seven hectares. According to witnesses, there are between one and two hundred criminally insane cases in the Carbó-Serviá ward, which measures twenty-five by fifteen meters, with a yard in the back.
Ariel Hidalgo:	(caption notes that he was sent to Mazorra in 1981 for founding a political party) There you are in the yard while it is light out, with no place to sit. There is saliva, human waste, or God knows what else everywhere.
Lourdes Meluza:	Those who have been inside Mazorra assure us that psychiatric methods are used to break all arrested dissidents. However, the authorities deny that these methods are used for political reasons.
Dr. Eduardo Bernabe Ordaz:	(caption identifies him as Director of the Havana Psychiatric Hospital) But in Cuba, never, never, never. On the contrary, we act

rapidly and diligently on all diagnostic reports given by our hospital about any of our patients to find out if they are ill or not.

Lourdes Meluza: During the thirty years of the Revolution, thousands of patients have been admitted to Mazorra. It is not known how many were for the "disease" of opposing the regime.

Voices of inmates: One, two, one, two, very well. . . .

Lourdes Meluza: Cuban psychiatry does not involve psychotherapy or analysis. It follows the Soviet Pavlovian School.

Voices of inmates: One, two, Viva Fidel, very well. . . .

Lourdes Meluza: Drugs, electroshock, and rehabilitation work are the psychiatric treatments used at Mazorra and throughout the island. But the therapy of caring for rose bushes does not apply to all patients. Eugenio de Sosa received eighteen electroshock treatments at Mazorra.

Eugenio de Sosa: (caption notes that he was sent to Mazorra in 1971 for sending a message from prison) When I was given electroshocks, it felt like thunder, an explosion. Then I was unconscious. Later, since I had not been strapped down, my whole body convulsed twenty times.

Lourdes Meluza: Jesús Leyva Guerra received twenty-four electroshock treatments at the Jagua Hospital in Santiago de Cuba.

Jesús Leyva Guerra:	(caption notes that he was interned as a result of charges of illegal exit from the country, possession of foreign currency, and distribution of counter-revolutionary posters) The effects included swelling of the lower and upper extremities and burned temples due to the electroshocks. I did not recognize my family or wife, and I secreted blood through my penis.
Lourdes Meluza:	The man in charge of all wards for the criminally insane at Mazorra does not think that any errors have been made with political prisoners.
Bernabe Ordaz:	We have no information about the use of psychiatry for other than scientific purposes for the welfare of the mentally ill. These cannot be political prisoners because there aren't political prisoners in our society. We have prisoners who are terrorists.
Lourdes Meluza:	Here in the United States, before applying an electroshock, the patient is given an anesthetic or muscle relaxant. The patient does not feel anything. Electrodes are usually placed on both temples and the most frequent treatment uses 150 volts for half a second or less.
J. Leyva Guerra:	They gave us electroshock without anesthesia. I never was given anesthesia.

174

Lourdes Meluza: Any sedatives?

J. Leyva Guerra: None. In those days, we received electro-shock every other day.

Eugenio de Sosa: I must have received eight or nine [through electrodes] on my head. All others were [administered] on different parts of my body.

Orlando Polo: (caption identifies him as President of a dissident movement known as *Ecopacifista*) I was surrounded by chronic cases, conditions for punishment were horrible, a medieval cell, cell nineteen.

Lourdes Meluza: Orlando Polo left Mazorra just a few days ago. He was sent to the Carbó-Serviá ward as punishment. Currently there are at least two other activists in Mazorra. This abuse of psychiatry is among the most recent concerns of human rights groups.

Armando Valladares: (caption identifies him as Director of the Valladares Foundation) They used to give two or three electroshocks in order to open a psychiatric file. When they were taken to court, it would appear that these young men had psychiatric problems, because only the mentally ill would disagree with the Revolution.

Frank Calzon: (caption identifies him as Director of Of Human Rights) Of course, this is one way that the Cuban government tries to cover up, by saying that there are no political prisoners.

Ricardo Bofill: (caption identifies him as President of the Cuban Committee for Human Rights) [Regarding] the cases of Julio Soto and Orlando Polo, these are two completely normal individuals because we know them. There is no doubt that these individuals do not have any psychiatric problems.

Lourdes Meluza: Here in Washington, several cases have caught the attention of the American Psychiatric Association, which has thirty-five thousand members. The Association has sent several letters to the Ministry of Health in Cuba, but they have not received an answer. The lack of cooperation could be an indication of guilt, according to a spokesperson for the American Psychiatric Association.

Ellen Mercer: (caption identifies her as spokesperson for the American Psychiatric Association) All psychiatrists are horrified by the use of psychiatry for political purposes. We will continue pressuring Cuba on this issue until they respond as openly as the Soviet Union.

Lourdes Meluza: Of Human Rights published a report on these violations and has adopted the case of Jesús Leyva, who received twenty-four electroshocks.

176

Frank Calzon: State security is the excuse. In other words, they are not using electroshocks as treatment. They are using them as methods of torture throughout the island.

Bernabe Ordaz: They send us patients. No other agency would interfere with a diagnosis given by the Havana Psychiatric Hospital.

Ariel Hidalgo: They said I had written a book against the Revolution. My torture was to leave me surrounded by men who could kill, rape, or do what they wanted with me. They wanted to drive me crazy.

U.S. DEPARTMENT OF STATE
COUNTRY REPORTS
ON HUMAN RIGHTS PRACTICES
FOR 1989: CUBA

(WASHINGTON: GPO, 1990), P. 531

. . . Several charges of confinement of political prisoners in psychiatric hospitals were reported in 1989. Four dissidents were confined in psychiatric hospitals, ostensibly for evaluation, for periods ranging from a few days to several weeks. None of the four reported mistreatment during their hospital stays. One, Julio Soto Angurel, leader of the José Martí Council of Independent Defenders of Human Rights and National Reconciliation, remained at year's end in the Havana Psychiatric Hospital, where he was confined after his arrest on October 8.

Following his release in 1989, Cuban Human Rights Committee member Jesús Leyva Guerra reported that security police detained him in July 1988 and then transferred him to the prison ward of the Gustavo Machín Psychiatric Hospital in Santiago de Cuba. Leyva said that he was forced to undergo psychiatric "treatment" and, after he began a hunger strike, was subjected to electroshock six times. . . .

HAVANA PSYCHOPATHY

EDITORIAL, *THE MIAMI HERALD,* 15 MAY 1990

In the play *Every Good Boy Deserves Favor*, Tom Stoppard's brilliant indictment of Soviet psychiatric abuses, a main character avers that dissidents in a totalitarian society are by definition "crazy" and thus deserve to be interned in psychiatric hospitals. The sane, reasons the character, do not risk suicidal confrontation with an all-powerful state.

But some, of course, do. Like their Soviet mentors in pre-Gorbachev days, Cuban authorities are using confinement to psychiatric hospitals as punishment for political dissidents. There, they are subjected to horrible treatment night and day.

Consider the example of Leandro Hidalgo Pupo. The young Cuban dared to stage a solitary protest at a boxing match in Havana two months ago. Before thousands of spectators, Mr. Pupo shouted denunciations of the Castro regime. He was brutally beaten for his unprecedented action and arrested. Last week it was learned that Mr. Pupo has been committed to the ward of Havana's National Psychiatric Hospital that is used to punish some of the Cuban government's political opponents.

Freedom House, a New York-based human rights group, has sent telegrams to the American Psychiatric Association (APA) asking it to intercede with Cuba on Mr. Pupo's behalf. The APA played an important role in the investigation of Soviet psychiatric abuses, but it lamentably has taken no active interest in Cuban cases.

The APA should do so with urgency. For while the Soviet Union is opening the doors of wards that once held patients subjected to arbitrary electroshocks, wet straitjackets, beatings by orderlies, and other barbaric practices, similar Cuban abuses appear to be increasing.

Freedom House has documented several cases. Americas Watch, another prominent human rights group, has also denounced Cuban psychiatric abuses. As it did when Cuba's Soviet mentors were abusing its dissidents, the APA should investigate Cuba immediately and place its findings before the United Nations Commission on Human Rights. Only the firmest protest will end Havana's officially sanctioned psychopathy.

RECENT DETENTIONS IN PSYCHIATRIC INSTITUTIONS

AMNESTY INTERNATIONAL

... According to Cuban law, detainees can be referred upon arrest to psychiatric institutions for tests in order to establish whether they are fit to stand trial. While this is a routine procedure and can in genuine cases benefit the detainee, Amnesty International fears that, in some cases, particularly political prisoners, the procedure may be open to abuse. In the case of the Havana Psychiatric Hospital, people not suffering any psychological disorder are often held together with violent psychopaths and seriously disturbed people, making their stay a very traumatic experience. . . . The following cases have recently been brought to the organization's attention:

Leandro HIDALGO PUPO

Leandro Hidalgo Pupo, aged about 20, was arrested in Havana on 23 February after he had shouted out anti-government slogans during an international boxing tournament in Havana. He was reportedly beaten and dragged away by police. Reports were received two months later that he was being held in the National Psychiatric Hospital in Havana in the special ward for prisoners called Sala Carbó Serviá on the grounds that he was suffering from "paranoid schizophrenia with moderate personality defects" (*"esquizofrenia paranoide con defectos moderados de personalidad"*). It is not known whether he is still being held there.

Juan BARZAGA SANTACRUZ

Juan Barzaga Santacruz was said to have spent nine months' in Sala Carbó Serviá after being arrested when participating in a demonstration of about forty people in Havana Central Park during which a statement was read out calling for democratic opening in Cuba. Barzaga is said to have sat down on the monument to Cuban national hero José Martí and refused to move until a plebiscite was held in Cuba. He is said to be a member of the national handball (*balonmano*) team.

Oscar PEÑA RODRIGUEZ

Oscar Peña Rodríguez, who was first delegate of the CCPDH [Cuban Committee for Human Rights] in the municipality of Mella, Santiago de Cuba, was reportedly detained on 12 December 1989 and taken to [the] Jagua ward of the local psychiatric hospital [*Editor's note: this in all likelihood is the Gustavo Machín Psychiatric Hospital in Santiago de Cuba, also known its pre-revolutionary name of Jagua*]. His wife was reportedly shown a document stating that he was being held there because of his *"peligrosidad"*, "dangerousness.". . . While there, he was said to have been held for sixty-five days in a punishment cell after allegedly trying to assist other patients. He was also reportedly threatened with electric shock treatment. He was later released but it is not clear when.

Luis Alberto PITA SANTOS

Luis Alberto Pita Santos, aged 43, is a member of the CCDHRN [Cuban Commission for Human Rights and National Reconciliation] and a former professor of Marxism-Leninism at the *Instituto Superior Pedagógico de la Educación Técnica y Profesional* in Havana. After having being briefly detained on two occasions in March and April 1990, he was arrested on 1 May 1990 following a search of his home during which many

182

documents were allegedly confiscated. He was charged with "clandestine printing" and following a hearing at the Marianao People's Court in Havana, he was provisionally released pending psychiatric reports. (This was reportedly the eighth time in four years that he had been referred by a court for psychiatric reports.) In July he was acquitted by the court on the grounds that he was *"en estado de enajenación mental"*, "in a state of mental alienation". In an open letter dated 27 August 1990, Luis Alberto Pita Santos said that the team of doctors in the Sala Carbó Serviá of the National Psychiatric Hospital where the tests on him were carried out treated him well and issued their opinion on 17 May 1990. He alleges, however that the version that was handed to the court was not the same one. He also wrote that, in the course of the investigations, several of his friends and relatives were questioned about his activities, including his human rights activities. Attached to the letter was a copy of a complaint he had presented to the police in which he accused twenty-seven people, including his former employers, party officials, judges and [the] staff of the National Psychiatric Hospital, of committing various offences ranging from preventing him from freely expressing his opinions to falsifying documents. On 28 August 1990, the day after he wrote the open letter, he was rearrested and taken to the State Security headquarters in Havana. On 3 September 1990, he was again transferred to the Sala Carbó-Serviá of the National Psychiatric Hospital where he was reportedly held for twenty-six days before being released without charge. It is not clear whether Luis Alberto Pita Santos has been in genuine need of psychiatric treatment or whether he has been persecuted because of his efforts to obtain justice for himself and others. Amnesty International is therefore continuing to seek further information on the case.

WORLD PSYCHIATRIC ASSOCIATION   **WELTVERBAND FÜR PSYCHIATRIE**

ASOCIACION MUNDIAL DE PSIQUIATRIA   **ASSOCIATION MONDIALE DE PSYCHIATRIE**

President: Costas Stefanis (Greece), Dept. of Psychiatry, Eginition Hospital, 74 Vasilissis Sophias Av., 115 28 Athens, Greece	Secretariat: Dept. of Psychiatry, Kommunehospitalet DK-1399 Copenhagen K
Vice-President: Jochen Neumann (G.D.R.)	Denmark, Europe
Secretary General: Fini Schulsinger (Denmark)	Teleph.: 45 1 93 85 00, ext. 3390
Treasurer: Niels Reisby (Denmark)	Telefax: 45 1 32 42 40
Associate Secretaries: Jorge Alberto Costa e Silva (Brazil), Melvin Sabshin (USA)	

Professor Eusebio Mujal-Leon
Department of Government
Georgetown University
Coordinator of Human Rights
Box 2160 Hoya Station
Washington, D.C. 20057

20 February 1989

Dear Professor Mujal-Leon,

In reply to your telegram of 19 January 1989 appearling for us to intercede with the Cuban government due to confinement to a psychiatric hospital of human rights activist Jesus Leyva Guerra, I have to inform you that the WPA's procedural rules for processing complaints of abuse of psychiatry demand that complaints are examined in collaboration with the WPA Member Society in the country in question.

As the WPA has no Member Society in Cuba, we cannot examine the complaint appropriately.

With my best wishes,
Yours sincerely,

Fini Schulsinger
Secretary General

184

V
BIBLIOGRAPHY

INTERVIEWS

Adela Bahamonde Cervantes, 17 April 1990.

Esteban Cárdenas Junquera, 27 April 1990.

Juan Manuel García Cao, 8 June 1990.

Amaro Gómez Boix, 11 March 1990.

Reina González, 24 April 1990.

Elena Granados, 23 April 1990.

Nicolás Guillén Landrián, 13 April 1990.

Ariel Hidalgo Guillén, 13 April 1990.

Lily Machado, 24 April 1990.

Orestes Martínez Haydar, 4 May 1990.

Samuel Martínez Lara, 9 July 1991.

Teresa Mayans, 11 April 1990.

Marcos Miranda Morales, 18 April 1990.

José Morales Rodríguez, 11 April 1990.

Georgina Perera, 11 March 1990.

Orlando Polo González, 11 March 1991.

Rafael Saumell, 18 November 1990.

Andrés Solares Teseiro, 12 April 1990; 6 June 1990.

Julio Vento Roberes, 30 July 1990; 21 August 1990.

Eduardo Yanes Santana, 27 April 1990.

AFFIDAVITS

Esteban Cárdenas Junquera, 6 December 1990.

Eugenio de Sosa Chabau, 10 July 1990.

Juan Manuel García Cao, 1 July 1990.

Reina González, 24 September 1990

Amaro Gómez Boix, 6 November 1990.

Nicolás Guillén Landrián, 4 October 1990.

Lily Machado, 5 July 1990

Teresa Mayans, 28 January 1991

Marcos Miranda Morales, 21 November 1990.

Andrés Solares Teseiro, 4 July 1990.

Julio Vento Roberes, 18 October 1990.

Eduardo Yanes Santana, 6 July 1990.

SOURCES

Alfonso, Pablo. "Fuentes: Recluído por Vocear contra Castro." *El Nuevo Herald* (*The Miami Herald*), 10 May 1990.

Almendros, Nestor and Ulla, Jorge. *Nobody Listened.* New York: Cuban Human Rights Film Project, 1988. Film.

Alvarado, José Luis. Written Statement, 9 May 1990.

Americas Watch. Press Release, 31 March 1989.

_____. Press Release, 7 April 1989.

_____. *Human Rights Activists behind Bars in Cuba.* New York: Americas Watch, July 1989.

_____. *Cuba: Jailing the Human Rights Movement.* New York: Americas Watch, March 1990.

Amnesty International. *Report 1983.* London: Amnesty International, 1983.

_____. *Torture in The Eighties: An Amnesty International Report.* London: Amnesty International, 1984.

_____. *Political Imprisonment in Cuba.* London: Amnesty International, 1986.

_____. Urgent Action News Release. 25 September 1986

_____. *Cuba: Political Imprisonment—An Update*. London: Amnesty International, January 1988.

_____. *Cuba: Recent Developments Affecting the Situation of Political Prisoners and the Use of the Death Penalty*. New York: Amnesty International, September 1988.

_____. *Political Imprisonment in Cuba: A Summary of Amnesty International's Recent Concerns*. London: Amnesty International, December 1989.

_____. *Cuba: Arrest and Imprisonment of Human Rights Party Members*. London: Amnesty International, June 1989.

_____. *Report 1989*. London: Amnesty International, 1989.

_____. *Medical Concern: Dr. Samuel Martínez Lara (Cuba)*. London: Amnesty International, November 1990.

Bahamonde, Adela. Written Statement, 28 April 1989.

Balmaseda, Liz. "The Mind of a Prisoner: The Case of an Exiled Activist Fuels Charges of Abuse in Cuban Psychiatric Hospitals." *The Miami Herald*, 25 October 1989.

Barnhart, Edward R., et. al., eds. *The Physicians Desk Reference*. Oradell, New Jersey: Medical Economics Company, 1989.

Bloch, Sidney, and Reddaway, Peter. *Russia's Political Hospitals: The Abuse of Psychiatry in the Soviet Union*. London: Victor Gollancz, Ltd., 1977.

_____. *Soviet Psychiatric Abuse: The Shadow over World Psychiatry.* Boulder, Colorado: Westview Press, 1985.

Camejo, Mary Jane. *Human Rights in Cuba: The Need to Sustain the Pressure.* New York: Americas Watch, January 1989.

Chardy, Alfonso. "Dissidents Arrested in Havana." *The Miami Herald*, 5 April 1989.

"Conferencia Nacional de Instituciones Psiquiátricas." *Revista del Hospital Psiquiátrico de la Habana* IV 2(April-June 1963): 207–251.

Coordinating Committee of Human Rights Organizations in Cuba. Press Release, 6 December 1990.

"Cuba Dumped Mental Patients on U.S., Psychiatrists Charge," *The Washington Post*, 14 October 1980.

Cuban Committee for Human Rights. "Informe de los Observadores del CCPDH que Concurrieron Al Jucio contra los Activistas Elizardo Sanchez, Hubert Jerez e Hiram Abi Cobas Nuñez." Manuscript, 1989.

De las Pozas, Ramon C., Merino, Norma, and Calzadilla, Luis. "Consideraciones para una Historia Natural de los Cuadros Depresivos (Considerations toward a Natural History of Depressive Disorders)." *Revista del Hospital Psiquiátrico de la Habana* XXI 1(JanuaryMarch 1980): 47–53.

De Sosa Chabau, Eugenio. "The Interrogation." *In a Place without a Soul: The Testimony of Former Cuban Political Pris-*

oners. Washington: United States Information Agency, March 1985.

_____. "A Witness to Cuban Tyranny." *The New York Post*, 1 November 1984.

_____. Interview with Lourdes Meluza, 1990. Part of "Psychiatric Abuse in Cuba," a news series by WLTV-TV, Miami.

"Ex preso muere ahorcado en hospital." *El Nuevo Herald* (*The Miami Herald*), 15 March 1990.

Garrido Ojeda, Juana. Statement to the United Nations Commission on Human Rights, 1 November 1988. Reprinted in Bofill, Ricardo, ed., *Cuba 1988: Situación de los Derechos Humanos*. Miami: Comité Cubano Pro Derechos Humanos, 1989.

Gastil, Raymond D., editor. *Freedom in the World 1982: Political Rights and Civil Liberties*. New York: Freedom House, 1982.

Gedda, George. "Office Seeker, Free Market Advocate, Loses in Rare Cuban Election." Associated Press wire report, 6 March 1989.

_____. "Testing Cuba's Limits: One Dissident's Quest for Free Expression." *Foreign Service Journal*, May 1990, pp. 24–28.

Gershman, Carl. Statement by the United States Representative to the Third Committee on Items 94 and 97, Human Rights and Scientific and Technological Developments and Torture and

Other Cruel, Inhuman or Degrading Treatment or Punishment, Press Release USUN 157-(83), 25 November 1983.

Gómez Boix, Amaro. "Persistencia de la Oscuridad." *El Nuevo Herald* (*The Miami Herald*), 10 February 1989.

_____. "Cuba: El Electroshock como Arma Política." *El Nuevo Herald* (*The Miami Herald*), 11 February 1989.

Government of Cuba. Ministry of Justice. "Certificacion de Antecedentes Penales: Angel Quiñones González." 18 August 1986.

_____. Judgement of 24 July 1975, Court of Crimes against the Security of the State, Havana, Cuba, Judgement number 177/75, Case 25/75.

Gralnick, Alexander. "Public Health and Psychiatric Care in Cuba: A Personal Report." Typescript, 1987.

Grogg, Patricia. "Builders of Hope." *Cuba International*, 1/89, pp. 26–29.

Havana Psychiatric Hospital. Certificate of Discharge, Case of Javier Roberto Bahamonde Masot. 21 January 1983.

"Havana Psychopathy." Editorial, *The Miami Herald*, 15 May 1990.

Hentoff, Nat. "The Sadist as Revolutionary." *The Village Voice*, 1 July 1986.

Hidalgo Guillén, Ariel. Written statement, 16 April 1990.

_____. Interview with Lourdes Meluza, 1990. Part of "Psychiatric Abuse in Cuba," a news series by WLTV-TV, Miami.

Hidalgo Portilla, Gualdo. Written Statement, 18 July 1990.

Human Rights Watch. *The Persecution of Human Rights Monitors, December 1989 to December 1990: A Worldwide Survey.* New York: Human Rights Watch, December 1990.

International Association on the Political Use of Psychiatry. "Should the Soviet Psychiatric Association Return to the World Psychiatric Association?" Pamphlet, International Association on the Political Use of Psychiatry, 1989.

Leyva Guerra, Jesús. Interview with Lourdes Meluza, 1990. Part of "Psychiatric Abuse in Cuba," a News Series by WLTV-TV, Miami.

Lowenstein, Roger. "Loyal Marxist Languishes in Cuban Jail for Writing on Privileged Ruling Class." *The Wall Street Journal* (International Edition), 5 June 1985.

Medvedev, Zhores and Medvedev, Roy. *A Question of Madness: Repression by Psychiatry in the Soviet Union.* New York: Random House, 1971.

Mendoza, Sandor. "A la Sombra de un Evento." *Aurora* 7 (September-October 1987): 10–14.

Nightingale, Elena O. "The Problem of Torture and the Response of the Health Professional." In Gruschow, Janet and Hannibal, Kari eds. *Health Services for the Treatment of Torture and Trauma Survivors.* Washington: American

Association for the Advancement of Science, Directorate for Science and Policy Programs, 1990

Ojito, Mirta. "Cuba suspende visitas de Cruz Roja a presos," *El Nuevo Herald* (*The Miami Herald*), 30 June 1990.

Ordaz Ducungé, Eduardo Bernabe. Comments on Arnaldo Torriente Gutierrez, "Trabajo Clínico de Observación de Procesados," *Revista del Hospital Psiquiátrico de la Habana* V (July-August 1964).

Peñate Fernández, Juan. "El Testimonio de un Cubano [The Testimony of a Cuban]." *El Miami Herald* (*The Miami Herald*), 25 August 1981.

Perlin, Michael L. "Patients Rights." In Klerman, G.H., et. al., *Psychiatry*, Volume Five: *Social, Epidemiological and Legal Psychiatry*. Philadelphia: J.B. Lippincott, 1986.

Polo González, Orlando. Interview with Lourdes Meluza, 1990. Part of "Psychiatric Abuse in Cuba," a news series by WLTV-TV, Miami.

Preston, Julia. "Castro's Clamping down Again." *The Washington Post*, 22 October 1989.

Ramirez, Antonio. "Cuban Teacher Jailed by Revolution He Supported." *New York Teacher*, 1 September 1986.

Regalado, Tomás. "El Sobrino de Nicolás [The Nephew of Nicolás]." *El Miami Herald* (*The Miami Herald*), 12 October 1983

Ritchin, Stephen J., et. al. *Human Rights in Cuba: Report of a Delegation of the Association of the Bar of the City of New York.* New York: Association of the Bar of the City of New York, July 1988.

Sakharov, Andrei. *Memoirs.* New York: Alfred A. Knopf, 1990.

Salas, Luis. *Social Control and Deviance in Cuba.* New York: Praeger, 1979.

Santiago, Ana E. "Ecología de Cuba Avanza al Desastre, Dice Experto (Ecology of Cuba Heading towards Disaster, Says Expert)," *El Nuevo Herald* (*The Miami Herald*), 14 November 1990.

Schanche, Don A. "Cuban Rights Crackdown, Psychiatric Abuses Told." *The Los Angeles Times*, 28 January 1989.

Schulsinger, Fini. Letter to Eusebio Mujal-Leon, 20 February 1989. Of Human Rights Correspondence File.

Simon, Gilbert I., et. al. *The Pill Book*, Fourth Edition. New York: Bantam Books, 1990.

Solares, Andrés. Written statement, 8 June 1990.

Soyu, Migdalia, Perera Horta, Jorge L., and Alonso Rodríguez, Alexis. "Violaciones Disciplinarias de los Pacientes en el Servicio Psiquiatra Forense [Disciplinary Violations by Forensic Psychiatric Service Patients]." *Revista del Hospital Psiquiátrico de la Habana* XXV 4(October/December 1984): 507–516.

"Sumario del 17 de Enero de 1989." In Ricardo Bofill, editor. *Resumen del Informe Anual de 1989 Sobre la Situación de los Derechos Humanos en Cuba.* Miami: Cuban Committee for Human Rights, 1989.

Treaster, Joseph B. "Cuban Rights, Even Today, Are Not So Libre." *The New York Times*, 19 January 1989.

_____. "Cuba is Reported to Arrest Three Human Rights Leaders." *The New York Times*, 7 August 1989.

United Nations Centre for Human Rights. *A Compilation of International Instruments.* New York: United Nations Publications, 1987.

_____. *Status of International Instruments.* New York: United Nations Publications, 1987.

United Nations. Economic and Social Council. Commission on Human Rights. *Consideration of the Report of the Mission which Took Place in Cuba in Accordance with Commission Decision 1988/106.* Forty-fifth Session, Item 11, E/CN.4/1989/46.

United States Department of State. Bureau of Human Rights and Humanitarian Affairs. *Human Rights in Castro's Cuba.* Washington: Department of State, 20 May 1986.

_____. *Country Reports on Human Rights Practices for 1989.* Washington: Government Printing Office, February 1990.

United States Pharmacopeial Convention, Inc. *United States Pharmacopeial Dispensing Information.* Volume II: *Advice for the Patient: Drug Information in Lay Language.* Ninth Edition. Harrisonburg, Virginia: George Banta Company, 1989.

Valero, Roberto. "Psiquiatría y Política en Cuba [Psychiatry and Politics in Cuba]." *El Miami Herald (The Miami Herald)* 12 July 1981.

Valladares, Armando. *Contra Toda Esperanza.* Barcelona: Plaza & Janes, Editores S.A., 1985.

_____. *Against All Hope.* New York: Alfred A. Knopf, 1986.

Weiner, Barbara A. "Treatment Rights." In Brakel, S.J., Parry, J., and Weiner, B.A., *The Mentally Disabled and the Law.* Chicago: American Bar Foundation, 1985.

Weiner, Richard D. "Electroconvulsive Therapy." In Volume Two of Kaplan, Harold I., and Sudok, Benjamin J., eds., *Comprehensive Textbook of Psychiatry.* Fifth Edition. Baltimore: Williams & Willkins, 1989.

Zaldívar Batista, F. Mario. Written Statement, 3 July 1990.

VI

INDEX

Freedom House

Freedom House is an independent nonprofit organization that monitors human rights and political freedom around the world. Established in 1941, Freedom House believes that effective advocacy of civil rights at home and human rights abroad must be grounded in fundamental democratic values and principles.

In international affairs, Freedom House continues to focus attention on human rights violations by oppressive regimes, both of the left and the right. At home, we stress the need to guarantee all citizens not only equal rights under law, but equal opportunity for social and economic advancement.

Freedom House programs and activities include bimonthly and annual publications, conferences and lecture series, public advocacy, ongoing research of political and civil liberties around the globe, and selected on-site monitoring to encourage fair elections.

Of Human Rights

Founded in 1975 by a group of faculty and students at Georgetown University, Of Human Rights is an independent nonprofit organization that collects and distributes information about the human rights situation in Cuba.

FREEDOM HOUSE BOOKS

General Editor: James Finn

YEARBOOKS

Freedom in the World: Political Rights and Civil Liberties,
annuals from 1978-1991

STUDIES IN FREEDOM

Escape to Freedom: The Story of the International Rescue Committee,
Aaron Levenstein; 1983

Forty Years: A Third World Soldier at the UN,
Carlos P. Romulo (with Beth Day Romulo); 1986.
(Romulo: A Third World Soldier at the UN, paperback edition, 1987)

Today's American: How Free?
edited by James Finn & Leonard R. Sussman, 1986

Will of the People: Original Democracies in Non-Western Societies,
Raul S. Manglapus; 1987

PERSPECTIVES ON FREEDOM

Three Years at the East-West Divide,
Max M. Kampelman; (Introductions by Ronald Reagan and Jimmy Carter;
edited by Leonard R. Sussman); 1983

The Democratic Mask: The Consolidation of the Sandinista Revolution,
Douglas W. Payne; 1985

The Heresy of Words in Cuba: Freedom of Expression & Information,
Carlos Ripoll; 1985

Human Rights & The New Realism: Strategic Thinking in a New Age,
Michael Novak; 1986

To License A Journalist?,
Inter-American Court of Human Rights; 1986.

The Catholic Church in China,
L. Ladany; 1987

Glasnost: How Open?
Soviet & Eastern European Dissidents; 1987

Yugoslavia: The Failure of "Democratic" Communism; 1987

The Prague Spring: A Mixed Legacy,
edited by Jiri Pehe, 1988

Romania: A Case of "Dynastic" Communism; 1989

FOCUS ON ISSUES

*Big Story: How the American Press and Television Reported and
Interpreted the Crisis of Tet-1968 in Vietnam and Washington,*
Peter Braestrup; Two volumes 1977;
One volume paperback abridged 1978, 1983

Afghanistan: The Great Game Revisited,
edited by Rossane Klass; 1988

Nicaragua's Continuing Struggle: In Search of Democracy,
Arturo J. Cruz; 1988

La Prensa: The Republic of Paper,
Jaime Chamorro Cardenal; 1988

The World Council of Churches & Politics, 1975-1986,
J. A. Emerson Vermaat; 1989

South Africa: Diary of Troubled Times,
Nomavenda Mathiane; 1989

The Unknown War: The Miskito Nation, Nicaragua, and the United States,
Bernard Nietschmann; 1989

*Power, the Press and the Technology of Freedom:
The Coming Age of ISDN,*
Leonard R. Sussman; 1989

Ethiopia: The Politics of Famine; 1989

*The Imperative of Freedom:
A Philosophy of Journalistic Autonomy*
John C. Merrill; 1990

*Racing With Catastrophe:
Rescuing America's Higher Education,*
Richard Gambino; 1990

*Soviet Propaganda
As A Foreign Policy Tool,*
Marian Leighton; 1990

Ireland Restored: The New Self-Determination
Vincent J. Delacy Ryan; 1991

*After the Velvet Revolution:
Vaclav Havel and the New Leaders of Czechoslovakia Speak Out*
Tim D. Whipple, editor; 1991

AN OCCASIONAL PAPER

General Editor: R. Bruce McColm

Glasnost and Social & Economic Rights
Valery Chalidze, Richard Schifter; 1988

Peace and Human Rights in Cambodia: Exploring From Within
Kassie Neou with Al Santoli; 1990

About The Authors

Charles J. Brown holds a Masters Degree from Indiana University and currently is completing requirements for the Ph.D. He is a Project Coordinator for the Washington Office of Freedom House.

Armando M. Lago holds a Ph.D. from Harvard University and is President of Ecosometrics, Inc., of Bethesda, Maryland. He is a member of the Board of Directors of Of Human Rights.